Tim,

Here is hoping that all of
the important relationships
in your life are working
relationships.

Regards
John Chisholm

Working Relationships

John Chisholm

*Managing Successful Relationships in Business and in Life
Using EQ and the Art of Difficult Conversation*

Published by JC Consulting; Kansas City, MO

Working Relationships: Managing Successful Relationships in Business and in Life Using EQ and the Art of Difficult Conversation

by John Chisholm

Copyright © 2019 John Chisholm
Published 2020 by JC Consulting

Paperback ISBN: 978-1-7342139-0-4
e-book ISBN: 978-1-7342139-1-1

Kansas City, MO
Website: johnchisholm.com

Cover design by George Estrada
Interior design by Dale Jimmo
Proof edit by Elizabeth Johnson

Printed in the United States of America

CONTENTS

PART THREE
Maintaining Healthy Relationships

PART FOUR
Appendix: Checklists & Worksheets

INTRODUCTION

Personal Business

One of the oft-repeated lines from the movie *The Godfather* is spoken by Michael Corleone to his brother Sonny. "It's not personal; it's strictly business." That line is almost as famous as it is untrue. All business is personal. Successful businesses—even unsuccessful ones—are founded on relationships that develop between companies and their customers, between employers and their employees, between business partners, coworkers, and colleagues. Personal relationships can be an important business tool, but they are just as important in every other aspect of life. Face it, life is all about personal connections—relationships with family, friends, and even with strangers. Maybe the most important relationship you'll ever have is with yourself. Do you like yourself ? Trust yourself ? Understand yourself? Are you deceiving, cheating, or overindulging yourself ? Are you clear about your life goals and daily objectives? Your experiences in past relationships will likely color your relationships going forward. Your success in business and in life depends on your ability to read other people's signals and react appropriately to them.

Church Fights

For eight years, I was a pastor in a nondenominational group that planted churches throughout the country. Each newly planted church required time to take root and grow, and as each congregation neared a hundred people in attendance, that church became viable, able to pay its bills and stable enough to hire full-time staff. I noticed as each new church reached viability, a pattern emerged. Conflict often ensued between the church-planting pastor and a main donor or a key elder, divergent personalities battling for control of the new church's direction. This is what we called a church fight. When differing people each believe that God is on their side, it makes for an interesting dynamic that can lead to some intense conversations. Because I had an aptitude and a willingness to step into church fights, I was often called in to help sort things out. I found there were usually three driving reasons for a church fight. One was a lack of role clarity—what was the role of the founding pastor, the elder, the donor? Secondly, there was often no clarified vision for where the church was headed. Thirdly, those involved didn't know how to conduct difficult conversations. They avoided what they needed to talk about, which inevitably led to blowups.

I was approached by a church member who was a business consultant for one of the largest accounting firms in the country. He had an office in the same community as my church group. He noticed the work I was doing with churches in the area and admired my skill set. He thought I could be useful in support of the family businesses he served. After all, similar dynamics affect both church congregations and family businesses. For both, relationships become strained when folks don't know how to effectively talk about problems. He asked me if I would be interested in working with him, serving his family business clients. I was ready for a transition, and so, I became a consultant.

Business Consulting

Plumbers fix leaks. Mechanics fix cars. Business consultants fix businesses. There are operational consultants, IT consultants, financial consultants and others with various expertise. A consultant may work with clients on strategy, planning, or problem solving. He might help clients develop business skills and knowledge regarding topics that range from designing a business model or a marketing plan to determining which marketing techniques are most effective and how to best implement them. A small business consultant brainstorms with clients to produce practical results and enhance strategic thinking. He advises, coaches, mentors, and teaches skills. Consultants share valuable insights that can boost internal creative thinking. Business consultants not only have academic and theoretical expertise, they may have practical experience working with leading companies in order to implement change. If you want to learn about best practices in areas such as tech or management, consultants can be a good source. They offer a fresh perspective. In-house people are sometimes too close to a situation and don't have the proper perspective to examine the bigger picture. Management consultants are experts at fostering change in organizations. If a company is rife with internal squabbling, bringing in a consultant can smooth feathers and ease tensions. Good business consultants blend practice and theory to deliver value to any struggling company, making them a natural choice for conducting training courses or daylong presentations for businesses.

As a management consultant and executive coach, I help clients create success through personal development in areas of strategy, communication, and team building. I also help them clarify and articulate vision while investigating root causes of self-sabotaging behaviors like procrastination and distraction. I help clients find answers from within themselves. I help them work through conflict and tackle hard conversations. I've learned to be a good listener. I'm adept at spotting weaknesses and identifying ways to turn them into strengths. I make the effort to learn my clients' professional strengths and weaknesses and their personal stories in order to fully understand all aspects of their businesses, past and present. I ask my clients to tell me what's working, what's not working, what things were like when business was booming, as well as when and where it all started to go wrong. Along the way, my clients usually divulge personal hopes and dreams, and I use their stories to help them achieve their goals. My job is to listen and absorb information and then come up with specific, actionable steps they can follow to get on track. Maybe they need better processes. Maybe they need higher performing people. Maybe a few key players need to learn how to get along and stop sabotaging themselves and others. Whatever the strategy, I help companies grow by teaching them to operate more efficiently.

I am often hired by firms when there is strain between executive partners that is affecting their business model. Over the years, I have added to my portfolio numerous testimonies of people succeeding in difficult conversations after applying the skill sets I've taught them. I've seen businesses and families literally transformed. I've been able to help people see their way through difficulty and find successful win-win outcomes time and again. When others are in conflict, I am skilled at facilitating solutions. But when risk is high and I am spinning in a swirl of negative emotions, it can be a challenge even for me to remember and use the skills I've learned.

A Difficult Conversation

I often think back to a specific conversation I had years ago that not only ran off the rails, it crashed terribly. Though painful, that conversation became a springboard that launched my consulting career. At the start of my career, I was partnered with a good friend and business mentor, the same church member who'd invited me to serve his family business clients. We went to the same church, had many of the same goals, and I looked up to him. Before long, we were running three successful businesses together—our consulting partnership, a store that sold clothing and merchandise for the University of Illinois, and a business that sold medical lasers internationally. Like any business, we had our ups and downs. The laser business was stumbling, and for a time I worked many hours without taking a salary. Eventually, we broke through and there was money to distribute. My business partner made a unilateral decision regarding the best way to distribute that money, a decision I didn't agree with. It wasn't what I had in mind. In fact, I took some offense at his decision. I knew I needed to confront him regarding my feelings. We needed to have what I knew would be a painfully difficult conversation. Not only were we friends, we were partners in three separate businesses, entwined on so many personal and professional levels that, if the conversation didn't go well, our lives would be quite different at the end of it.

When I started my consulting practice, I didn't coach people on how to have difficult conversations. I'd taken some training on the topic, but it hadn't been my focus. I still had much to learn. As the conversation began, my resentment and indignation crept to the surface. When I expressed my feelings bluntly, my business partner became offended that I was offended. Feeling uncomfortable with a perceived attack on his ability, he clicked into business mode, taking on a professional demeanor, cold and distant in his responses, which only served to offend me more. The conversation wasn't going well, but instead of slowing things down so we could hear each other out, I pushed and picked up speed. One of the things I now coach my clients is to slow a crucial conversation down. When things start to derail, take a break. I did the exact opposite. Our dialogue pinched a few of my own insecurities, and because I didn't like what I was feeling, I wanted the conversation to end. I suddenly wanted our business relationship to end. I wanted our friendship to end. I wanted it all to end. I wanted out. I was done.

I've since learned that issues regarding compensation are rarely about money. The core issue for me was tied to personal value and the way I viewed myself. I didn't feel I was being valued by my partner the way I should be. I told him I wanted out of our business interests and that I wanted to separate our personal lives. He, of course, became even more offended. Things just unraveled from there. We stopped doing consulting work together. I ended up switching churches, sold my part of the clothing store, and got out of the laser business. Looking back, I realize we should have consulted a third-party facilitator. We might have found a way to mitigate feelings of personal offense before making such major business decisions.

If I could give my younger self some advice, I would tell myself to slow down the conversation and not let emotions drive it off track. Emotions are an important part of any difficult conversation because they bring needed information to the table, but they should never be allowed to steer. Letting my offense lead the conversation caused me to make some big decisions that should have been given more fore-thought. That conversation was a painful turning point that ultimately worked for my good, but I regret the way I handled it. A couple months after our difficult conversation we each owned up to our part of the conflict, though our friendship never fully recovered. We asked one another for forgiveness for any lingering offense, and then we went down different professional paths.

We all struggle with hard conversations. I used that particular difficult conversation as a catalyst for learning more about how to have them. Hard conversations became a focus of my consulting practice, and it was then that my professional career really took off.

Relationship Investment

I don't believe it's possible to overstate the importance of relationships, whether in business or marriage, with family or friends, neighbors or strangers. Relationships are a reliable source of joy and inspiration and connectedness, making them, I'd say, the truest measure of success. I come from a large family which includes six brothers and a sister. When I was young, I was outgoing and precociously friendly. Whenever I saw an opportunity to share with a neighbor, I did, spilling everything that came to my mind. I was eager to tell everybody what was happening at the Chisholm household. Sometimes I embarrassed my family members, and my parents had to be careful about what they said around me for fear I might share it with the neighbors. Eventually, my father sat me down and talked to me about it. He appreciated that I wanted to be friendly but informed me that I was straining relationships at home. He explained to me that there was a difference between being friendly and being good at relationships. That has always stuck with me.

Over the years, I've learned it's worth spending the time it takes to make a relationship inventory. I often encourage clients to compile a list of the important relationships in their lives, to make note of which are going well and which are strained. What underlies the relationships that are going well? What's happening in those relationships that makes them positive? Consider the relationships that are strained. Why aren't they going as well? I encourage you to do the same. Write out what works in your good relationships and what's at the heart of your strained relationships. You'll find important information there.

Stephen R. Covey in his book *Seven Habits of Highly Effective People* coined the term, "relational bank accounts." Like their monetary counterparts, relational bank accounts include deposits and withdrawals. Think of a relational deposit as a connection point, an affirmation or meaningful interaction that you bring to a relationship. A withdrawal might be a verbal conflict or offense or maybe even an asked for favor, something that is a cost to the relationship. We need to be consistently aware of relational equity. Withdrawals are unavoidable, so continual deposits are necessary. Sometimes we do things that affect others in a positive way. Sometimes we do things that affect others negatively. It's in the nature of any relationship that there will be deposits and withdrawals. You can't make a withdrawal from a bank account if there's no money in that account. Without equity, you're out of luck, in arrears, bankrupt. Same for relationships. If you keep making withdrawals without balancing deposits, the relationship will go bust. That's how relationships are destroyed. You need to ask yourself again and again, *what is the status, the state, of my relationships? How much equity is in each account?* If a relationship is important, you should be looking for ways to make regular deposits as an investment for the future.

> *The only way a relationship will last is if you see your relationship as a place that you go to give, and not a place that you go to take.* —*Tony Robbins*

Keep in mind that a deposit is defined by the party you are trying to invest in, not by you, not by what you think is important for the other person. If you want to invest in a relationship, you have to consider what is meaningful and important to the other side so you can deposit your time and energy there. This is especially true for strong personalities and high performing individuals who have a tendency to focus on the end result and miss the impact on relationships along the way.

I used to work closely with the University of Illinois Athletic Department, and I once had the incredible opportunity of watching a closed basketball practice with the varsity coach. What I saw was startling. Coach Bill Self was a knowledgeable and charismatic man, but after witnessing one of his closed practices, I could only conclude that he was also one of the scariest, meanest men I'd ever seen. He was intense, intolerant, sometimes screaming as he barked orders. He pulled players' jerseys and pushed them into proper position. Sometime later, when he announced he was taking a job at the University of Kansas, I thought the locker room at U. of I. would be full of student athletes celebrating his departure. Actually, the opposite was true. Many on the team, saddened by the coach's leaving, actually wanted to follow him to Kansas so they could remain under his tutelage. I asked around, wanting to know why those kids were so devoted to a guy who was so intense and who made such deep demands. I was told about all the deposits he made with his players. He invited them to family dinners, making each team member feel a part of his family. He sat with each of them and listened to their individual stories. He asked what they wanted out of basketball, from the University, from life. He committed himself to working on their behalves, to helping them achieve their athletic and personal goals. He invested his resources in them, and then he spent that equity by asking so much from them.

At times, I have found it necessary to say challenging things to my children. Sometimes I may even come across as intolerant. When I share things that seem harsh, not all warm and fuzzy, I'm asking for a withdrawal, and I have to be sure there's equity in that account, in the relationship between us, in order to make those withdrawals. I am purposeful about it, spending the acquired equity in such a way as to strengthen the relationship and ultimately help them to become healthy adults.

We all need to be good bankers as it relates to relationships. We need to make deposits in order to spend equity, and we have to be careful about how and when to make necessary withdrawals.

EQ for Dinner

Some of the tools I now employ I learned back when I was a young parent. I have six children today, but back when we had only four, my wife and I placed great value on dinnertimes together. We still do, but back then, I can't tell you how often one of the kids spilled milk, and it drove me crazy. I wanted dinnertime to be meaningful for the whole family, for all of us to be connected and enjoy a picture-perfect experience together. But milk kept being spilled, and it frustrated me to the point that I would start barking, upset, bordering on angry at something the kids didn't intend and didn't really understand.

Later, my wife let me know that my reactions were not helping the family. I thought, hey, I have the right to be frustrated. They're spilling milk. I remember my wife asking what I hoped to accomplish, because the way I was responding wasn't helping. This forced me to look inside myself. Why was I so frustrated about spilled milk? I talked it out with her, digging for what drove my reaction, because I already understood the kids' behavior. Kids spill milk, right? No great mystery. I eventually realized it wasn't the kids or the spilled milk that was frustrating me. It was what I believed about the sanctity of dinnertime and how my role as a parent was to make things run smoothly. My frustration stemmed from my perception of myself as a parent and my memories of the dinnertime experiences I had as a child. It wasn't until I identified the beliefs driving my frustration that I was able to manage my reaction and see spilled milk for what it truly was
—a simple accident. If it was about the spilled milk, then I could've changed the drinking glasses, put covers on them, maybe changed who sat next to whom, but I didn't consider any of that because I was so frustrated and angry.

> *Everything that irritates us about others can lead us to an understanding of ourselves.* —Carl Jung

The problem was an identity issue. At its deepest level my reaction was related to my beliefs about dinnertime and my insecurities as a parent. The spilled milk poked my insecurities, and all at once my beliefs were driving a negative emotion that wasn't helping any-one. What did I want? What was my goal for dinnertime? I wanted a fabulous bonding experience, everyone feeling connected, all of us discussing how we were doing and how our day had gone, but that was ruined because of the underlying beliefs that I brought to the table.

My problem was rooted in self-awareness, a key component of emotional intelligence, which is sometimes referred to as EQ (as

opposed to IQ). All relationships, whether business or personal, feed
and are fed by emotional intelligence. My experience investigating
ways to strengthen EQ has played an important role in my personal
life as well as my career as a management consultant and executive
coach. From experience, I've learned a vital insight that, properly ap-
plied, can help you thrive and succeed. Here it is: Emotional intelligence and difficult conversations are separate but synergistic building
blocks that effectively strengthen relationships, which are every day
and everywhere. In other words, difficult conversations feed and flow
from emotional intelligence in ways that support and strengthen a
healthy process for building and sustaining relationships, which are
the key to success in business and in life.

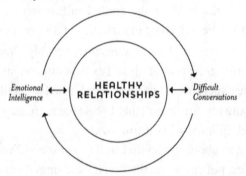

If you bought this
book, or are even just
browsing through it,
chances are you want
something more from
your life. My long ex-
perience as a business
consultant tells me that
no matter what specific
things you think you want, relationships, both personal and business,
are the key to achieving them. This book is offered as a road map and
a game plan for establishing healthy relationships. What follows is a
breakdown of the important components of emotional intelligence as
well as a practical guide for effectively navigating difficult conversations. My hope is that you will learn to identify and isolate components
of your EQ, use and strengthen them through the art of difficult conversation, and apply the insights you gain to build and sustain healthy
relationships. The process is circular. Each element strengthens the
others. Some of the insights I'll be sharing may sound simplistic on
paper, but in truth, the achievement of healthy relationships is every
bit as difficult as life itself. And likewise, the rewards that flow from
healthy relationships can be as transformative and joyful as anything
in your life.

PART ONE

The Need for Emotional Intelligence

Chapter 1

EQ—What It Is and Why It's Important

If you follow current trends in business or in education you've no doubt heard the term emotional intelligence, or EQ. It is different from IQ, which represents abilities such as visual and spatial processing, knowledge of the world, reasoning, and memory. EQ, on the other hand, is a measure of a person's emotional intelligence, a person's ability to perceive, control, evaluate, and express emotions.

In 1990, two professors, John Mayer and Peter Salovey, did groundbreaking research on the topic of emotional intelligence and the ability to measure it. They offered evidence of an emotional quotient that measures the ability of individuals to manage and analyze their own emotional responses as well as the emotional responses of others. Their research showed that the ability to manage yourself and the way you relate to others may be more relevant than was first believed, perhaps even more relevant than standard IQ. In 1995, *New York Times* science writer Daniel Goleman's book *Emotional Intelligence: Why It Can Matter More Than IQ* shared findings in terms the average person found accessible. The book was a best seller, and people started talking about the ramifications of EQ. It helped bring awareness of emotional intelligence and made it a hot topic in areas ranging from business management to education.

In professional settings, it used to be that people were judged primarily by their intellect. A person's IQ could open doors of opportunity in the workplace. Today, that is shifting. There are many reasons why the spotlight is moving away from IQ and towards EQ. One of the primary reasons is that a great deal of information is now available with a simple keyboard stroke. Search engines make information available to pretty much everyone, and artificial intelligence even makes it accessible at the sound of your voice. So, hiring is no longer focused solely on who is the most intelligent. Employers are looking at who is most suited to lead. Research shows a person's EQ can help determine one's ability to do just that. EQ, as it relates to professional leadership, can be distilled into two primary components: the ability to relate well to others, and the ability to manage oneself. The sector perhaps most impacted by EQ is education. Many educators find it helpful for creating healthy learning environments. They know they can do little to affect a student's IQ but, because EQ is neither predetermined nor set in adolescence, educators can affect one's EQ dramatically.

My daughter-in-law recently graduated from Harvard Business School. She wouldn't have been accepted if she hadn't proven herself to be a resourceful person with a bright mind, but in addition to the skills and understanding you'd expect in a class of MBA intellectuals, she told me that a large focus of her studies was concerned with the understanding and self-actualization involved in *how* she performed. She was startled by how pervasively EQ influenced and drove the way her professors structured the classroom as well as the content they were presenting. They were interested in knowing whether she could lead and relate well to others, important components of EQ. Major businesses like Google invest great sums of money in learning how to attract and retain talented people. High IQ individuals are valued, but businesses also need people who can effectively lead. They need people who can rally a department, an organization, or a team to accomplish a purpose. IQ alone doesn't determine one's ability to do that. The business world is awakening to the need for people with high EQ. The good news is, regardless of your stage in life, you can further develop and strengthen your EQ.

An ability to understand and manage emotions greatly increases your chances of success in life. Your ability to understand and manage your emotions in positive ways—to relieve stress, communicate effectively, empathize with others, overcome challenges, and defuse conflict— allows you to recognize and understand what others are experiencing emotionally. For the most part, this is a nonverbal process that both informs your thinking and influences how well you connect with others. IQ can help you get into college, but it's your EQ that will help you manage stress while facing your final exams. IQ and EQ coexist in tandem and are most effective when they build off one another. Emotional Quotient is the ability to sense, understand, and effectively apply the power and acumen of emotions to facilitate high levels of collaboration and productivity. In any business environment, EQ is important because it helps you leverage your awareness of emotions for effectiveness in the workplace.

> *Emotional intelligence is not the opposite of intelligence, it is not the triumph of heart over head—it is the unique intersection of both.* —David Caruso

The concept of emotional intelligence has evolved over the years, from its inception back in the 1930's as something called *social intelligence* to *emotional strength* in the mid-20th century, to the current term, *emotional intelligence*. You may have met people who are empathetic and easy to talk to. Those people can be considered to have a high EQ. You've probably also met people who are self-centered and oblivious to other people's feelings. Those people might be considered to have a low EQ. The ability to understand what motivates others, to relate in a positive manner, and to build stronger bonds with others in the workplace inevitably makes those with higher emotional intelligence better leaders. An effective leader can recognize the needs of his people, so those needs can be met in a way that encourages higher performance and workplace satisfaction. An emotionally savvy and intelligent leader is also able to build stronger teams by strategically utilizing the emotional diversity of team members to benefit the team as a whole.

Whatever business model you employ, you are in the people business. No one, as the cliché goes, is an island. Ultimately, you have to work effectively with your boss, your colleagues, and your clients. And that's just the people at the office, never mind your loved ones at home. Your ability to motivate, regulate, and apply passion and focus to a problem is critical for your personal and professional growth. In order to strengthen your emotional quotient, it's necessary to examine the five skill sets that comprise emotional intelligence. The first two, **social skills** and **empathy**, concern the ability to relate well with others. The other three, **self-motivation, self-awareness**, and **self-regulation** are all about an individual's ability to manage internal emotional responses and external behavior. In the following chapters, I'll break down these five components of EQ and offer strategies for strengthening your emotional intelligence.

Chapter 2

Social Skills

Do you relate well to others? Are you friendly and approachable? Can you work effectively with others?

A key trait of people with a high EQ is that they are comfortable around others, even those who are difficult. They are also the people others feel comfortable around. They are approachable, accessible, and non-intimidating. They have the ability to connect with people. They do things *with* people, not *to* them. They look *at* people, not *through* them. In other words, they have strong social skills. Social skills are necessary in order to get along with others and to create and maintain satisfying relationships. They allow us to interact and communicate effectively with other people, including verbally (the way we speak to other people) and nonverbally (our body language, gestures, and eye contact). Almost every job requires social skills. Whatever business model you employ, you are all in the people business, which is why people skills are so important for effective leadership and management. If you work on a team, you need to be able to get along with others. If you work with clients, you must listen attentively to their questions and concerns. If you are a manager, you will be called upon to motivate employees. Even if your job does not involve interacting with others very much, you still need to possess a few socials skills in order to interact effectively with your employer or colleagues.

They may   forget what you said—but   they will never forget how you made them feel.   —Carl W. Buehner

There is a popular television show these days called *The Good Doctor*. The main character is something of a genius when it comes to diagnosing and treating serious illnesses and injuries. He also has a high functioning form of autism that limits his social abilities and negatively impacts his personal relationships. Because of his incredible expertise as a medical specialist, and perhaps because he's young and well intentioned, his colleagues and superiors graciously accept his awkwardness and overlook his occasional, emotional outbursts. The *Good Doctor* might lead one to believe that social skills aren't really essential. As long as you're the best in the world at what you do, as long as you bring a lot of creative energy or revenue to your business, being personable and socially skilled isn't all that important.

On Tv maybe. In the real world, not so much.

Social performance can affect success in any business, whether you're a CEO or an office drone, an accountant or an attorney, whether you're a butcher, a baker, or a candlestick maker. The truth is, social standards are different for Tv characters and singular performers like famous athletes, musicians, or celebrity chefs. If you can throw a hundred mph fastball or run a hundred yards in under ten seconds, if you can play an electric guitar like Jimi Hendrix or sing the blues like Janis Joplin, folks will more likely ignore your childish temper tantrums or rude behavior towards others. But consider that many highly skilled performers, particularly those who are self-centered, often have broken relationships in their personal lives, include multiple marriages and ongoing legal battles with their management teams. The cost of poor social skills can be steep, even for the financially successful.

We all stand to benefit from developing our social skills in order to thrive and succeed in relationships, both in business and in life. If you lack confidence as a social creature, don't worry. Social skills can be taught, practiced, and learned. You can behave with social confidence even if you don't feel it. Don't allow anxiety to hold you back. Make the decision to talk to new people and to enter into conversations even when you're feeling nervous about it. Over time, it will get easier and you'll quickly start improving your social skills. If you're uncomfortable with attention in a conversation, get familiar with open-ended questions that require more than a yes or no answer. That may open the door to invite the other person to keep the conversation going. Most people enjoy talking about themselves. Ask about a person's career, hobbies, or family. Show that you are interested in hearing what's being said. Offer compliments generously. Compliments are a great way to spark a conversation.

Another simple though often overlooked way to practice and reinforce your social skills is to show people you are approachable by remembering to smile. In the chaos of a workday, taking time to smile acknowledges the value you see in others, and it goes a long way toward building personal connections. Also, make a point of using a person's name in conversation and maintain eye contact. There is power in a person's name. It may seem like a given, but addressing people by name and looking them in the eye establishes a personal connection that can be transformational. If eye contact is daunting for you, or if remembering names is sometimes difficult, begin with the next person you meet. Practice your social skills in everyday, trivial conversation, and build from there.

Chapter 3

Empathy

Do you seek understanding or only to be understood? Do you have the ability to get outside of your own perspective and make room for others?

Empathy is about seeking to understand and connect with someone where they are. People with a high EQ understand that we all have different perspectives, different thought processes and different ways of looking at life, and they make room for that. They are not locked into a belief that their way is the only way. Too often, when our buttons are pushed, we react poorly because we subconsciously think in that moment that our way is the only way or the best way. People with a high EQ make room for the reality of diverse perspectives, and they place value in that diversity. They are able to set that information in front of them when their buttons are pushed, which diffuses their reactions and precipitates personal growth.

People with a high EQ understand that everyone is wired differently. Most of the people you come into contact with don't think or act like you or have your values. Understanding that others are different from you, and making room for that, strengthens your empathy. It's more than just a philosophical notion. It takes effort and energy to make room for different points of view and to pursue understanding.

Many times, our difficulty in working with others is tied to the fact that we are out of touch with how drastically different we are from each other. We don't understand why people view the world the way that they do or why they make the decisions they make.

After I graduated from the University of Illinois with a degree in psychology, I got my first real-world job selling gold and diamonds for a jewelry distributor. I worked for three years before being recruited by Pulsar, a sister brand of Seiko Watch Corporation. My father had been a Bulova watch salesman for thirty-five years before moving to Pulsar, and he helped get me the job. A few years later, a corporate decision was made to bring the entire salesforce of Pulsar to Tokyo for a sales meeting. I was nervous about the trip and somewhat clueless about cross-cultural dynamics. I'd never been outside the United States and was particularly concerned about the prospect of eating foreign foods. I decided to bring a large salami with me so I wouldn't starve. Yes, I was younger then, even younger than my age in some ways. On our first day, we were invited to a welcoming affair that included various food booths serving traditional dishes—teriyaki, sashimi, yakitori, tempura, and sushi. I was relieved to discover most of the foods were delicious. I was never even tempted to break open my salami. Later, we attended a celebratory banquet called a Sáke Barrel Ceremony, commonly performed at special events. Everyone dressed in traditional Japanese regalia, and the ceremony included the opening of a sáke keg with a wooden mallet. I'd never tasted sáke before but found it quite agreeable. Afterward, we were served a special meal that required the use of chopsticks. I sat at a table with three other American salesmen, four Japanese executives, and no silverware whatsoever. My American tablemates joked about our inability to use the chopsticks effectively, but over the course of the meal we got better at it.

Perhaps the sáke played a role in my playful behavior. Laughing and pointing my chopsticks aimlessly, I sometimes stabbed my food as I enjoyed the meal and the camaraderie. After a time, one of the Japanese executives asked to speak with me away from the table. He escorted me to a private corner and let me know, in no uncertain terms, that my behavior was disrespectful and offensive. He was deeply distressed by my actions. *Never point chopsticks at another person,* he told me, and *never stab your food. It is quite insulting to everyone sharing the meal.* I apologized profusely before returning to the table, humbled and humiliated. I'd been clueless to the cultural customs and sensitivities of my tablemates. I hadn't considered that their thoughts and feelings could be so different from my own experience and understanding. I was a guest, and my behavior, inadvertent though it was, offended my hosts. I committed right then and there to never place myself, or others, in such a situation again.

> *We do not see things as they are, we see things as we are.*
> —*Anais Nin*

Cross-cultural sensitivity isn't only important while visiting foreign lands. It is sometimes necessary when dealing with your next-door neighbor or the boy who bags your groceries or your classmates or colleagues or even your in-laws. Often referred to as a melting pot, America is really more of a tossed salad made up of a wide variety of lifestyles, faiths, and cultures—African and Asian, French and Finnish, Greek and German, Hispanic and Irish and Jewish and so many more. A multicultural society inevitably results in cross-cultural dynamics that can become problematic as we bump up against each other's values and beliefs.

You'll hear me say this again and again—life is about relationships. In order to build cross-cultural relationships, it's important to first understand our own cultural norms. Why do we think the way we do? Why do we act the way we do? What does politeness look like for us? How do we handle disagreements or build friendships and relationships? What personal traits are most important in our cultural heritage? Consider fashion, body language, eye contact, work ethic, gender roles, personal space, foods and holiday traditions, attitudes toward rules and authority and family life.

The standards and beliefs of people from other cultures or other parts of the world may seem foreign to us, as ours no doubt seem to them. Awareness of that fact, and respect for it, is crucial to building relationships in cross-cultural environments. We have to be open to the idea that the way we see the world and the norms we hold close are not the same for others. We must be prepared to embrace and adapt to unfamiliar norms if we want to sustain and grow cross-cultural relationships. It's important to be open to the reality that others do life differently. It's helpful to cultivate a desire to grow in understanding of our differences and to learn to be comfortable in the ambiguity and awkwardness of uncertainty, perhaps even stepping on some toes or having our toes stepped on, as we work to build and strengthen relationships.

Some skills that help build cross-cultural understanding include self-awareness, curiosity, comfort with ambiguity, mindfulness, and empathy, all important attributes of emotional intelligence. Empathy is about being other centered, which at times requires culturally sensitivity. Strangers can be intimidating, even frightening, particularly strangers from other cultures or with vastly different worldviews, but our individual differences are really just entry points, opportunities for learning and discussion about ourselves and others, in other words, about life itself, which is where joy and success are found.

At the heart of empathy is listening. If you work to effectively listen to others, you'll able to retrieve the data you need to understand them. Maybe you have family members, coworkers, or friends who are challenging. If you take the time to sit with them and ask them a bit of their story or their perspective on a common topic, you'll find your ability to empathize with them increases. Keep in mind, you're not trying to evaluate their story or judge their position. You're just trying to understand it. Connection is the goal. When you understand someone, a connection forms, and from there, relationships can grow and thrive. Empathy is about seeking to understand others, and the truest way to learn about others is to listen to them.

When you talk, you are only repeating what you already know. But if you listen, you may learn something new.
—Dalai Lama

It's worth repeating. Listening—deliberate, active listening—is a crucial aspect of emotional intelligence. It is the key to difficult conversation, and it plays a vital role in healthy relationships. Listening is central to everything this book is about. It's so important that I will dig deeper into the power of listening as it applies to difficult conversations in a later section of this book.

Chapter 4

Self-Awareness

Are you in touch with your strengths and weaknesses? Do you know the impact you have on others, and can you manage that impact?

People with a high EQ are sensitive to who they are and the effect they have on others. Self-awareness is key to a person's ability to lead and to sustain successful relationships.

During my days as a pastor, a gentleman who was a clinical psychologist became part of our congregation. He was a very successful psychologist with a doctorate in counseling, and he enjoyed a thriving consulting practice that involved helping police departments around the country to choose suitable candidates as police officers. He used a battery of tests that helped him to evaluate the candidates. After I got to know him a bit, he suggested my pastoral team take some tests to see how he might be able to help us be more successful as pastoral leaders. It was a bit intimidating, but we trusted him, so we all took the Myers-Briggs Personality Inventory, and the Minnesota Multiphasic Personality Inventory. I was particularly fascinated by the Myers-Briggs instrument. It offered feedback and provided in- sight into my personality that made me feel as though someone had been following me around for years. I loved the instrument so much that I went out and got certified in administering it myself.

For me, perhaps the most insightful tool was the Minnesota Multiphasic Personality Inventory, referred to as the MMPI-2. It's an instrument that asks 567 true/false questions. *Do you like to watch buildings burn? Do you enjoy your bowel movements?* It sometimes repeated the same question in different ways. I've since learned that there are two different types of psychological instruments: self-reporting and projective. A self-report only tells you what you tell it. For example, the Myers-Briggs Personality Inventory asks if you like to be around people. If you reply that you do, the results may reveal you are extroverted. It's a self-reporting instrument that reflects back to you whatever you told it. A projective psychological instrument, on the other hand, tells you things you never told it. Our criminal court system uses the MMPI to evaluate mental health and competency to stand trial. It told me things about my psychological health that I never told it, things I didn't even know. The test revealed that I had an elevated score on what was known as the Pd scale, the Psychopathic Deviant scale. I know. Sounds bad, doesn't it? You can imagine my shock and concern. Given that I was a pastor at the time, I needed to know what the test results meant. When I asked for an explanation, the counselor told me that items on the Pd scale were designed to tap into complaints about family and authority figures in general. He asked me if I'd ever been treated poorly by someone who had authority over my life, and if I'd ever made the decision to step out from under that authority. Turns out, I'd been in several such situations. The counselor thought I might have unresolved anger issues in relation to some of those experiences. I didn't think so, but when he offered to spend time exploring some of those events with me, I agreed. He initiated a process that became an eye-opening journey, one that brought healing to my heart regarding past traumatic experiences with which I'd been completely out of touch.

As I explored the feelings and memories connected to those past events, I was able to get more connected with my true self and my place in the world. It was uncomfortable, even painful at times, but it was a process that bore much fruit in my life. I'd been too long out of touch with my emotions, not knowing how to process anger or hurt in healthy ways. I'd rarely taken time to examine my thoughts or feelings. Counseling brought a self-awareness that allowed me to better relate to my emotions. I learned to manage my heart, to process pain and anger, and to better relate to other people's emotions. I'm appreciative of the impact those tests and the resultant counseling had on me. It made me a better husband, father, and pastor, and I believe it helped me become a more effective management consultant and executive coach. The experience underscored the importance of, and my need for, reflection and self-awareness. I wasn't able to effectively address issues that were holding me back until I was made cognizant of the problems. I understand now why it's so important to look inward as much as outward.

The best way to grow in self-awareness is to be open to feed- back, whether from a formal assessment or from those around us. In the business world, as in difficult conversations, giving and receiving feedback are critical tools. If you want to strengthen your self-awareness, professionally or personally, you have to learn to gracefully receive feedback from others. The key is to remember it's not about whether you agree with it or how it makes you feel. Feedback is often painful. The point of feedback is that you learn to receive and evaluate data in the interest of self-awareness and, ultimately, personal growth. All of us have blind spots. Being open to feedback is crucial. Without it, we simply cannot grow as far or as fast as we can with it.

Keep in mind, there is an important difference between knowing and agreeing. You want to know even if you don't agree. Teachability is a sign of maturity. If you have a teachable attitude, you will receive more helpful feedback and become more effective in your life and career.

It's very important to have a feedback loop, where you're constantly thinking about what you've done and how you could be doing it better. —Elon Musk

To grow and strengthen your self-awareness, ask three or four people whose opinions you value the following questions: *What things do you think I excel at? In what ways do I contribute positively to this team or relationship? In what areas do I still need to grow?* How do I negatively impact this team or relationship? Remember, this is a time to receive feedback, not respond to it. The better you are at receiving honest feedback, the more valuable feedback you'll receive, and the more people will be willing to give it to you. Reflect on their feedback for more than a day. You may not agree with all of it, but commit to taking a few weeks, months maybe, to really weigh the thoughts and opinions of the people you trust. Look for emerging themes and work over time to adjust your behaviors accordingly.

Another way to increase self-awareness is to try a new skill or put yourself in a challenging learning environment. Step into a situation where you are forced to grow or reach for something new. It will reveal facets of your personality that you may not be exposed to on a daily basis. Making a commitment to run a marathon or signing up for a business conference will put you in a position to learn and grow and stretch yourself, perhaps revealing how well you work with or relate to others. Afterward, take time to debrief or assess yourself and your performance. Don't be too hard on yourself but be honest, and work on making any necessary changes for the future.

Chapter 5

Self-Motivation

Do you take responsibility to be proactive and manage your energy? Can you effectively manage your passion and your time?

Too often people are dependent on the environment or outside factors for motivation, but those with a high EQ are able to find personal motivation. They are able to proactively take responsibility in order to bring their energy, passion, and focus to a given goal. They understand the most effective behaviors are driven from the inside out, not the outside in. That is an important component of EQ and a critical aspect of the way one deals with conflict. When things are difficult, there's a tendency to pull back or away from that situation. Having a strong sense of personal motivation helps one lean into the conflict, even when it doesn't feel good.

There is a well-known concept in psychology called self-efficacy. It refers to a belief that you can make a difference in the world, that you can change things or do something to impact life around you. That's important, because hopelessness can be crushing. If you find yourself in poverty or some other excruciating circumstance and you believe there's nothing you can do about it, without self-efficacy it's difficult, maybe impossible, to rise above your bleak condition.

People with a high EQ rally their energy and strength toward specific goals.

High EQ individuals hold goals for their careers, their relation-ships, and their personal growth. When their buttons are pushed or they are provoked in a difficult conversation, they don't lose sight of their goals. They are able to ask themselves, *what's the best response to help me get where I want to go?* They understand they are responsible for their motivation and can rally their focus and strength around those goals, and therefore act accordingly. If someone at work provokes an emotional response, they're able to quickly identify how their reaction might move them further toward or away from the goals they have in mind.

As a youngster, my son played soccer. He was in a park district league and one day he came home with a trophy that was two feet tall. I asked him what he did to earn such an impressive trophy, and he said it was for participation; everybody on the team got one. Sadly, that's not uncommon. Too many people believe the way to grow self-esteem is through trophies and indiscriminate praise. Society sometimes de-cides to hand out trophies to make folks feel better, but that's not the key to increasing self-esteem or self-efficacy, and it doesn't provide the opportunity for growth. The key to growth and self-worth is in learning to face and overcome challenges.

I once had the opportunity to coach a grade school cross-country team. The school my children attended could find no one willing to take the job. I'd run high school track back in the day, and I had some understanding of what was required, so when the school principal asked if I'd be willing to run the program, I accepted. The previous year, there were only eighteen kids on the team, and the school was unable to put seven athletes at the starting line who could finish a two-mile run. In my third year of coaching, we won the regional champi-onship and qualified for the state championship. That's of little conse-quence to you, I know, but it's a great memory for me. Anyway, in the second year of the program we had about seventy students on the team and we were starting to attract kids who weren't particularly athletic. There was a young lady who was a little overweight. She also had low self-esteem and only joined the team because her friends were on it. She was slow and couldn't run a quarter mile without stopping. Now, an important aspect of the program was that we helped all the kids set goals relative to who they were, and we tracked those goals. Some of the students wanted to lower their time, while others just wanted to run a little farther without stopping. This young lady's goals were to run a half mile without stopping, then to run a mile without stopping, and then ultimately, to try to run two miles without stopping. Those were her goals for the year.

As the season unfolded, she moved closer to her ultimate goal. One day she arrived at a meet believing it was her time. She said to me, "I think this is the day. I'm going to run two miles without stopping." She'd never done it before, though she had reached her goals of running a half mile and a mile without stopping. Two miles was a much bigger reach, and I wasn't sure she could do it, but she believed she could, and that made all the difference. Off she ran, and sure enough, she was doing it, a half mile, a mile, a mile and a half. She was running and she wasn't stopping, and suddenly, the whole team seemed to understand what was happening. This was it. She was going to finish the race without stopping. The entire team lined the track, shouting encouragement and yelling her name, and when she crossed the finish line, the whole team cheered as though she'd just won the race. They were celebrating that she'd accomplished her ultimate goal. As her teammates swarmed her, she was bent in pain and out of breath, and I waited until she'd recovered before going over to give her a big hug. The memory is still strong with me. She looked me in the eye, smiling through her tears, and said, "I did it!"

That's where self-efficacy comes from. It comes from learning to overcome difficulty by setting goals and accomplishing those goals. People who are effective leaders, when difficulty comes, they believe they can do something about it. They believe they can work through, around, and over barriers, whatever it takes.

So, growing in self-efficacy is important, but how do you do it? Self-efficacy doesn't come by being handed a big trophy or accolades. It comes from experiencing success and realizing effective outcomes, and it requires balance. If you put someone who is not ready into an incredibly difficult situation, self-efficacy can be destroyed. Yet the right amount of pressure can offer a person the opportunity to learn how to deal with difficulty. It can offer an avenue for working through stress and finding ways around barriers in order to experience success. And when people experience a little success, it empowers them to handle more difficulty and achieve even more success.

You can grow or strengthen your self-motivation by attempting things you don't presently feel confident about. Maybe you don't feel capable of cooking French cuisine or playing a musical instrument. Sign up for a lesson and give yourself the chance to thrive. Purposefully put yourself in a challenging situation that forces you to lean in and press through difficulty. Taking on new challenges allows you to experience the positive things that can happen, even as it helps you to build resiliency and perseverance in the face of failure.

If you're feeling even braver, go to your boss or team leader and ask for a new, challenging task or project. Perhaps you can suggest a new initiative, or maybe there is a focus group you can start, or a team project with another department. Strengthen your personal motivation by setting goals and going after them.

Chapter 6

Self-Regulation

Can you manage your heart, your emotions, and your words? More importantly, can you manage those things in a way that produces healthy outcomes?

High EQ individuals don't fly off the handle whenever something doesn't go their way. They know how to manage their emotions. Whatever they are thinking, they don't just blurt it out. Whatever they are feeling, they don't just act it out. They manage to control their thoughts and feelings, because it's not okay to lose your cool at work or with people you care about. In order to work well with others, self-regulation is a crucial tool.

Rarely are our emotions a result of something that has happened to us. They are a result of what we believe about what has happened to us. As you know, emotions often feel like they are out of our control. Sometimes life does too. That's because too often, we view the world as a jumble of random things happening, good and bad, but the reality is, although we may not always be able to choose what happens to us, we can choose how we respond. The key is to develop the capacity to do so. That's what self-regulation is. It's developing the capacity to manage your self-talk, manage your belief systems, and ultimately, your emotions. Self-management is the heart and soul of EQ and a crucial tool for productive business.

People with a high EQ take responsibility for their emotions and manage them.

People with a high EQ don't feel destined to respond in a certain way. When provoked, they don't immediately think, *that person made me react like this. What was I supposed to do?* They understand they are not victims. Instead, they know they have the power to decide how to respond. That is both liberating and challenging. The choice of how to respond still needs to be a healthy one. It can take time to learn the best ways to respond strategically and emotionally. People with a high EQ recognize that they are responsible for how they react and know it's sometimes necessary to step away from a situation in order to process the most effective way forward.

It's important to acknowledge that you have buttons people can push. We all do. A button is a sensitive area in your life that, when provoked, sets you off, and let's face it, usually in an uncomfortable or embarrassing way. People with a strong or high level of emotional intelligence are not without buttons, but they know how to identify those sensitive areas and are purposeful in dealing with them. Their goal is to turn those buttons from trigger points into opportunities for growth. When someone sets them off, they know to look inward instead of accusingly at the one provoking them. They own the problem and set their focus on removing their vulnerable buttons. In competitive environments, perhaps when company profits and promotions are on the line, a coworker under pressure might try to sabotage your shot at moving up by intentionally pushing your buttons. How you manage yourself—how you respond when someone provokes you—makes all the difference. If you find your buttons being pushed at work, your reaction may not only reflect poorly on your level of professionalism or your promotion eligibility, over time it can jeopardize your job security. So, how do you remove those pesky buttons? It takes time, but the first step is to recognize and own them.

We all have areas in our lives with potential for growth. Conflict, regardless of the type, can be an excellent flashlight on those areas. It shouldn't be overlooked, and it can't be overstated that the first step in dealing with an area that is easily provoked is to acknowledge that it exists. People with a high EQ not only know that such areas exist they actively try to address the reasons they exist. When someone pushes a button, they see the trigger as an opportunity to further grow and learn more about themselves. A provocation doesn't unbalance them. Instead, they see it as a mile marker or indication of where they've been and where they are going. The next time someone pushes your buttons, don't allow your emotions to take the wheel. Ask yourself what's going on inside, and then challenge yourself to take ownership of that area. You might not have control over a situation, but you do have control over how you respond to it. Developing your EQ not only helps you manage a right response to conflict, but it can also give you the strength and ability to reduce the number of vulnerable buttons you have in the first place.

Too often, people don't understand the purpose of emotions or why they arise. They think emotions emerge from nowhere, and because of that, they allow their emotions to take over. Emotions help us process life. They provide insight into what's going on internally. They are a crucial component of EQ and are important in difficult conversations, so they should be expressed, but they are not designed to lead. Again, it's not what happens to us that causes emotion. It's what we believe about what happens to us that causes our emotions. People with a high EQ, when faced with an emotionally charged situation, know to look inside themselves for answers as to why they are reacting in a particular way. They also take responsibility for managing that reaction. They look at their own belief systems and address things at a root level.

Anyone can become angry, that is easy; but to be angry with the right person, and to the right degree, and at the right time, for the right purpose, and in the right way, that is not within everybody's power and is not easy. — Aristotle

Let's focus for a moment on anger, perhaps the most common emotion, at least the most often expressed. People sometimes think their expressions of anger are due to their emotional sensitivity, as though flying off the handle were a sign of a high EQ. It's not. Anger is a secondary response. The primary emotion feeding it usually involves pain or disappointment. When we can't articulate our pain, we quickly turn to anger, thinking we're in touch with our emotions, thinking that anger is a perfectly normal and natural way to express our feelings. In fact, there is such a thing as righteous anger. We can be legitimately angry about unjust offenses or wanton cruelty, but most often, and especially in difficult conversations, anger is a secondary response to some sort of pain—pain that we don't know how to constructively process or perhaps pain that we haven't even identified yet. It's easier to express anger than it is to articulate pain. Sometimes we don't even know what we're feeling or why, because we lack the emotional intelligence, so we let loose our anger. We're more used to anger, more comfortable with it. Anger can feel good. It emboldens and empowers. But we get no insight from anger unless we know where it's coming from, whether the cause is some past hurt or current offense. Once hurt is laid bare, we can address the issue beneath the emotion, and then we're better able to direct our anger and even control it. When pain is expressed, anger dissipates. Only then can we can begin to unlock the real issues that need attention. Expressing anger is easy. We sometimes do it thoughtlessly, but expressing disappointment or pain, and dealing with the reasons for it, requires emotional awareness, which is key to a strong EQ and foundational to healthy relationships.

Chapter 7

Managing Emotions

To most people, feelings and emotions are synonymous—two words with the same meaning. The truth is, although they are dependent upon each other, emotions and feelings are distinct and separate things. Emotions are involuntary responses to external or internal events, and they are generated subconsciously. Feelings, on the other hand, are subjective experiences driven by conscious thought. In other words, you can experience emotions without feelings, but you cannot have feelings without emotion.

Emotions are not problems to be solved. They are signals to be interpreted.   *—Vironika Tugaleva*

Emotions help us survive, avoid danger, make decisions, and understand others. Perhaps more importantly, they help others to understand *us*. Other people's emotions affect us and trigger our own emotions by virtue of the information they convey. We feel comfortable and safe when we sense calm in others. When we see someone's face express fear, we quickly look for danger nearby. You sometimes hear people speak of emotions as if they come out of nowhere then drain away. But emotions come from somewhere, and they serve a purpose. In order to manage emotions, it's helpful to understand their purpose, where they come from, and the belief systems that drive them. By altering your belief systems, you can shift your emotions and better manage your responses to external situations. High performing persons exhibit better self-control and are better able to manage their emotions. In business, if you cannot manage your own heart, you're going to have a hard time managing others.

Managing your emotions is a matter of self-regulation, which is crucial to effectively navigating difficult conversations and strengthening relationships.

Emotion is the body's response to what's happening around you, bad things and good things. They're important in helping you process events in your life. You don't want to ignore or deny them. Emotions also lock in experiences. When a positive thing happens and there is an outburst of emotion, it releases chemicals in the brain and body that can make what happened hyperreal in a concrete way. I still clearly remember the moment my youngest son walked for the first time. It was a joyous occasion that is now seared into my heart. Of course, what is true in a positive way is also true in a negative way. When profoundly negative things happen, strong emotional responses lock that experience into our minds and memories as well. If, God forbid, we were to lose a loved one, grief would come unbidden in its own time as we processed that loss. We can't speed up grief. It's a part of life, yet we sometimes do a poor job of relating to or expressing our grief. It's important to understand that grief is a process driven by belief systems, a way of dealing with the reality of loss and the fact that someone integral or connected to us is now gone. We need to process that, and that takes as much time as it takes.

When something important happens that is unwanted or painful, a reaction is inevitable, an outburst perhaps, and we may need to debrief with someone about it. So, we instigate a conversation, and the more we talk, the more negative emotions are stirred up. We fall into a cycle that makes it hard to talk objectively about the topic. The important thing to remember is that emotions are there to help us process, but they're not designed to lead. You may feel angry, and that's real and legitimate and important, but you shouldn't lead with anger in a conversation. That will only take you to unproductive places and bring impediments to strengthening a relationship. Emotions are a part of life, an essential part, and in difficult conversations they are an important part of the process, but you have to be careful not to let them consume the conversation, or the conversation will derail and fail. Manage your emotions and make room for them, but don't let them lead or control you.

It's helpful to remember the purpose of emotions. The subconscious mind communicates through the language of emotions so we're able to find pleasure, avoid pain, and maintain well-being. If you don't eat for a long time, it's not just your stomach that signals hunger. Your subconscious mind will send feelings that something is wrong, motivating you to look for food. Imagine if you were unable to feel hunger. You wouldn't know when your body was depleted of nutrients. You might become weak, suffer malnutrition, and die without ever being warned by your mind. Likewise, emotions arise from your subconscious mind to warn you and guide your decision making. They are there for a purpose beyond just creating drama in your life.

Nothing is positive or negative in and of itself. We consider something positive if it benefits us and negative if it harms us. Strictly speaking, no emotion is negative, because all emotions motivate actions that lead to needed outcomes. You might consider fear a negative emotion when it deters you from riding a fun roller coaster, yet you'd consider it positive if it helps you run from an attack of swarming bees. Positive emotions are the ones that make you feel good. Negative emotions are the ones that make you feel bad, yet emotions are primarily triggered by thoughts that arise from belief systems or an interpretation of external events. When an event happens, you attach meaning to it. It is this meaning that results in emotion, and it's important to recognize that the meaning you attach to events is partly innate and partly learned. The problem is that the attachment of meaning process is not completely conscious. That's why most people believe emotions appear out of nowhere and that they have no control over them. They haven't considered that their emotional state changes in part because they don't have enough emotional awareness, the awareness of situations and thoughts that trigger emotions. Emotions only appear to be automatic because people aren't plugged into the fact that those emotions are formed in the depths of their subconscious. They only become aware *after* emotions are triggered.

> *When awareness is brought to an emotion, power is brought to your life.*   *—Tara Meyer Robson*

Some people are more in touch with their emotions than others. Emotional awareness is a skill that can be developed through practice. The subconscious mind gathers information from the environment, sorts out facts, then decides the suitable emotion to be triggered in a given situation. The process is influenced by beliefs, by the thoughts that arise from those beliefs, and consequently, by the way you interpret an event. Some beliefs are genetically programmed, like the fear of falling, while others are learned. As you develop your emotional awareness, you'll be able to observe the thoughts that cross your mind as you experience certain events, and with practice, you'll come to know exactly what causes your emotional state to change.

Chapter 8

Controlling Emotional Responses

We learn about emotions from family and from our experiences growing up, but inherited belief systems are often unconscious and therefore harder to identify. Not all emotional responses are helpful. Take
hold of the ones that aren't and change them. That's the most important point I'm trying to make about emotional reactions: you can control them. Emotions can feel as though they've come out of nowhere.
They're strong and can threaten to overwhelm you, but the important
takeaway here is that emotions come from somewhere, and if you are
able to decipher where they're coming from and understand why, you
can manage them. Again, it's not what happens to you that causes
emotion. It's what you believe about what happens to you that causes
your emotional response.

Imagine police lights flashing in your rearview mirror. You're
speeding, in a rush to get somewhere and not paying attention, and all
of a sudden, flashing police lights appear behind you. You know you're
guilty and about to get a ticket, and a flood of negative emotion wash-
es over you. But if you've been going the speed limit and don't believe
you're at risk in any way, and all of a sudden there are flashings lights
back there, you probably won't feel the same fear. You might wonder
if the cop is after someone else, or maybe why he's pulling you over

when you haven't done anything wrong, but you won't experience the same degree of negative emotion. Your immediate emotional reaction will be dictated by what you believe, which may have little to do with the actual data at hand—your speed, his intentions. Lights in your rearview mirror don't cause a negative response. It's what you believe about those flashing lights that causes your reaction. Once you understand that your belief system drives your emotions, you can learn to control them. As you evolve and grow, you can also change your belief system to make yourself more proactive. The more self-control you display, the more effective you'll be in difficult conversations, which will strengthen your relationships. Learn to manage your own heart and you will become a more effective leader.

Your emotions help you process what is happening to you. The good news is, emotions imprint into your psyche the experiences of intensely positive events. The bad news is, the same holds true for intensely negative emotions and events. The important thing to remember is that emotions are not designed to lead. In a strong emotional state, you run the risk of making bad decisions. Identifying emotions can help you build better relationships. Awareness of your emotions can help you express your feelings more clearly, avoid or resolve conflicts, and move past difficult feelings more easily.

Expressed emotions dissipate feelings. Unexpressed emotions continue to mount and may lead to an explosion of feelings. Emotions feel large on the inside, and you might fear expressing them because they could blow up. The reality is just the opposite. Holding onto emotions and not expressing them is what leads to a blow up. Express your emotions in a controlled way and offer your anger or your sadness or whatever emotion you're feeling as a puzzle piece, so you can talk about issues that need discussion. In a difficult conversation it's essential to make room for emotion. You want to know what the other party is feeling. It's a puzzle piece, and when expressed, emotions will dissipate. If you don't make room for that, if you don't allow emotion into the conversation, you'll never get all the puzzle pieces. There may even be an emotional explosion. Don't be afraid to express emotion. Make room for it. Draw it forth.

When you make room for emotion, upbringing and personal

experience will likely come into play. Some of us have had traumatic experiences and things we've never processed. We think we're talking about a certain topic, and then fear steps in or anger rises up, and suddenly, emotions are whirling and fuses are lit, which is why a healthy process is so important. Sometimes it's necessary to take a timeout. Maybe something is said that touches a place of insecurity in one person, or one party expresses emotion and the other doesn't know what to do with it. You don't want to completely shut down or walk away. You want to take a bit of time to ask yourself what's going on. Why is this so hard for you or for the other person? It's tempting to take a no emotions allowed approach. You might think a difficult conversation would be easier and safer that way, but it's not. Without properly expressed emotion, the process is even more volatile, and puzzle pieces remain out of reach.

I grew up in a home where emotions were frowned upon and crying wasn't tolerated. As I came into adulthood, I often didn't know what I was feeling. When I found myself in a meaningful relationship with the loving woman who is now my wife, I remember sometimes looking at her in wonder, thinking, *what exactly am I feeling right now?* Not only did I have trouble expressing my feelings because I didn't relate to the emotions underneath, I was also uncomfortable anytime emotion was expressed towards me. Think about that. If you're uncomfortable when someone expresses an emotion, who's got the problem? The answer is you. You've got a problem, and you'll need to dig deep in order to confront and deal with it.

I've coached too many business executives who have shared with me a similar experience while giving performance evaluations to employees. I've been told how disconcerting it can be when an executive gives pointed feedback to an employee and that employee starts crying, causing the executive to freak out a bit, thinking, *you're not allowed to cry. I'm just giving you feedback. Stop crying!* The truth is, a performance evaluation can be a matter of grave consequence to the employee receiving it. It's silly to think that wouldn't be an occasion for emotion. That's why it's important to make room and even encourage other parties to express their feelings. It can make for an incredibly meaningful conversation that can drive change in an employee's behavior. If emotion isn't allowed, the employee may feel distanced, less connected to the organization. In short, make room for emotion, reflect emotion, affirm emotion, draw it out. When it's expressed appropriately, emotion will dissipate, and then difficult conversation can effectively cause puzzle pieces to appear. In that way, relationships can be strengthened, and business will improve.

As a management consultant I'm hired by organizations to address internal conflict that is often so severe it's affecting business. Sometimes I'm told solutions have been attempted, but there's just no way to fix the problem. I say, watch me. I know healthy process gets puzzle pieces on the table. Healthy process allows difficult conversations about painful events between individuals who have never talked about them before, and all of a sudden, I'm listening to strong-willed, gifted personalities speaking with quavering voices about something incredibly painful, maybe from years or decades before, yet they've never talked about it, and they're having a hard time expressing their emotions. As a third-party facilitator, I employ healthy process so clients can reach places and achieve successes they've never been able to before.

One of my more significant consulting engagements occurred early in my career. I was referred by an accounting firm to one of their clients, a construction contractor with seven partners. The senior ranking partner owned fifty-one percent of the company. Six other partners held the remaining shares. I was called in to manage a strategic planning session. They were blue collar, volatile folks with a construction worker's rough vocabulary. The intensity in the room quickly went from zero to sixty. One said something, another disagreed and threw words back at him, and next thing I knew, the one came across the table at the other, ready to throw punches. Having been in pastoral ministry for eight years, this dynamic was new to me. The rough language and intensity were startling.

They needed help. Their process was flawed, which was putting their company at risk. I had to get them to understand how important process was, so I took time to customize a few hats, blue ball caps with the word DIALOGUE across the brim, yellow ball caps with the word CAUTION, blank white caps, and construction worker hardhats.

I explained that the blue hat represented the importance of healthy dialogue. It was to be used for simple exploratory conversation, to discover why someone said something, why a particular word was used, to ask for examples or clarification, or because someone wanted to better understand what someone else was talking about. The white hat meant all was steady and on track, no problems or concerns. The yellow hat meant caution, look out, someone was about to say something that others might not like. The hardhat was for when the conversation got to that place where things usually broke down and the sky was falling.

The seven partners sat at a conference table, each with the four hat choices in front of them. I explained that we were all going to do the exercise together. When someone changed to a different hat, we all had to put on the same color. I facilitated the discussion, and slowly the partners caught on, engaging with one another while wearing the appropriate hat. They began with the white hats, until someone wanted to spend time exploring what was said. Then we all traded to blue and dialogue ensued. When someone felt the need to make a comment that he knew would be upsetting, he reached for the yellow hat. Everyone followed suit, and we all looked at each other with our yellow hats on. When something was said that made others angry, the hardhats came out, signaling things were about to get rough. The hope was to get back to yellow, maybe to blue, so we could get more puzzle pieces on the table, and then eventually back to our white hats. The process slowed things down, made everyone more self-conscious, and at the same time more sensitive to one another. The activity forced everyone to recognize emotional responses from others and to control their own. It resulted in a dramatic breakthrough that underlined how important process is. All seven partners were able to manage a difficult conversation they'd never before been able to have.

Chapter 9

Identifying and Changing Belief Systems

While earning a degree in psychology, I learned a bit about cognitive theory. People behave and emote as they do because of the belief systems that fuel their behaviors and emotions. Remember all that spilled milk at my dinner table when I was a young parent? I wanted to change my reactions to that problem, my emotions and behaviors, so I needed to address the belief systems that drove them. I needed to analyze the thoughts in my head, the feelings in my heart. Why was I so frustrated? I saw the spilled milk as a reflection of my parenting. If I was a good parent, then dinner would go smoothly and there would be peace in the kingdom. But there was no peace in the kingdom, therefore, my parenting skills were sadly lacking and I was a lousy parent, and that frustrated me, causing me to react strongly—and badly. You might be thinking, *hey, no kidding, Sherlock*, but in the moment, I didn't see the connection.

How do you identify belief systems? How do you change them? Full disclosure—it isn't easy to uncover or tweak the belief systems that drive our behaviors and emotions. But there are some import- ant questions you can ask yourself. *What is the catalytic event that is causing emotion?* That's step one: Identify the underlying cause. *What would my dinnertime scenario look like if seen through the lens of a camera?* First, this happened, and then that happened, and then came my response. An event or events happened, and then I started correcting my children. I raised my voice. I expressed anger and ultimately disrupted the entire meal. It would seem to a neutral observer that events outside my control caused my reactions. In the moment, it seemed that way to me as well. It felt like the spilled milk triggered my frustration, and therefore, I acted out. I was clueless until I examined the belief system that drove my emotional response and triggered my behavior, and then I was able to understand where all my frustration was coming from. It was all about my perception of myself as a parent. I didn't always feel well parented when I was a child, so I wanted to get it right for my kids. I felt at risk, not very good at parenting, and the evidence was in that spilled milk. My belief system about dinnertime and about parenting drove my negative emotion and behavior. Once I identified that belief system, I was able to work on changing it.

Belief systems are an important part of emotional intelligence and a tricky aspect of difficult conversations. The ability to shift your belief systems and regulate what's going on inside you can improve your life and make you a more effective business leader. It can be empowering to know that you are not restricted by what happens to you, that you can influence your own perception and understanding and thereby control your emotional responses.

Unfortunately, the way the brain is wired can make it difficult to implement belief system changes. A major culprit is something called *limbic lag*. There are two parts to our brains. One is the *neocortex*, the analytical center of the brain located in the front of the head. It processes, analyzes, and stores information for decision making and remembering. The other part is called the *limbic system*, which controls emotion and the involuntary systems of the body, including survival responses. When you feel threatened, these protective responses signal you to either defend yourself or run away. The limbic system doesn't have a memory like the neocortex. To the limbic system, there is no difference between yesterday and yesteryear, which explains why some childhood traumas can still trigger us so powerfully today.

The neocortex takes time to develop, but the limbic system is churning from birth. Every event and sight you take in as a baby is stamped with an emotional response. If it's good, the limbic brain wants to repeat the experience. If it's negative, the limbic system tries to avoid it. It is the limbic system that is most affected by beliefs and emotional behaviors. The limbic system can be negatively programed through traumatic experiences, say, growing up in a dysfunctional family. In order to change your automatic, emotional response alarms, you have to reprogram your brain by first discovering false beliefs and then replacing them with truth. Maybe you've been sabotaging relationships in your life by believing you don't need anybody. Your limbic system has learned that having needs in a dysfunctional family results in vulnerability, abandonment, isolation and pain. In order to survive, you may have developed a system of thought that leads you to subconsciously think, *I don't need anybody. If I don't need anybody, I'm not vulnerable. If I'm not vulnerable, I won't get hurt.* Of course, it's not true, but every time you experience feelings of vulnerability, your limbic system sends emotional warnings, signaling you to flee from possible pain.

Even trickier, the emotional side of your brain doesn't always agree with the logical side. This is called limbic lag because the limbic system is slower, lagging behind the logical neocortex. The limbic process happens automatically and subconsciously, so even after a painful or traumatic situation is over, the subconscious continues to believe what it feels. Even after you've discovered false beliefs (spilled milk makes you a bad parent) and know a new truth, there is a time lag between what your limbic system believes and what your neocortex has learned. The *limbic process* can take anywhere from days to years, but it gets shorter as you continue challenging false beliefs and traumatic memories. Old, automatic habits aren't shifted quickly or easily. Change happens one decision at a time. To break old habits and decrease the time of limbic lag, listen to what your mind knows, and do what is best or right rather than what your emotions tell you. It is comforting to know that there is a physiological reason why your feelings do not automatically line up with your rational thoughts. The limbic system makes it difficult for us to make changes that involve risk unless it feels it is safe. Change is possible, but it takes committed process to reprogram your brain by discovering false beliefs and replacing them with truth.

All personal breakthroughs begin with a change in beliefs.
                                                    —Tony Robbins

So, why is all this limbic lag stuff important? Because, as you be-gin to implement changes to your belief systems, you may feel wrong while doing the right thing, and it may feel right to do the wrong thing. Your limbic system will be stuck in its old ways for a while. As you work to get a new thought into place, it may not generate a right feel-ing yet, but if you let your emotions dictate your response, your new thoughts will be aligned with old feelings. Limbic lag will cause you to feel wrong doing the right thing. It may feel awkward or uncom-fortable. Brain science says it takes about twenty-one days to change a serious habit, that's three weeks to change your thought process. Limbic lag makes it more challenging to shift your belief systems, but it's worth learning to manage your emotional responses to events out-side your control. It's empowering, and it will set you up for success in the marketplace, at home, and in life. There are four important steps to changing your belief systems.

First, consider the situation you need to think through for the next time a particular event happens. For me, the situation included my being part of a family at dinnertime when milk was spilled. I mentally rehearsed it, visualizing what would happen, and I understood that what was going to change was not the event. The change would be in how I responded to it.

Next, consider your goals regarding your feelings. In my situation, the next time milk was spilled, how did I want to respond? Well, I want-ed to be more at peace. I wanted to be able to process what was happen-ing so I could consider changes to ensure it didn't happen again. I didn't want all the negative emotion. I didn't want all the frustration. The next time spilled milk happened, I wanted to be gracious with my language. I wanted to be at peace regarding my relationship with my children.

Step three is to consider behavior goals. Imagine the behaviors you want to see in yourself. My goal was to continue having a peace-ful, meaningful dinner, even though milk was spilled, and to calmly process things, to laugh and smile and accept that I hadn't ruined dinner or anything else.

Lastly, consider what new beliefs will drive your feelings goals and your behavior goals. The next time milk spills at my dinner table, what beliefs will allow me to remain at peace and be gracious and keep smiling? I'll need to embrace the belief that spilled milk at dinnertime is not the full measure of my parenting skills. If bad things happen while I'm parenting, that doesn't mean I'm a disaster as a parent. Maybe that's more than one belief; it's two beliefs, but it was the belief system that would drive the emotional response I wanted. That's the belief system I needed to integrate into my thinking and my life.

It's crucial to listen to your inner self and your logical mind. You may have thoughts like, *oh, that can't be it. That doesn't make sense.* I can't tell you how surprised I was to discover that spilled milk was somehow connected to the way I viewed myself as a parent. The idea that I saw dinnertime as a measure of my parenting skills, and spilled milk as a sign of my failure in that regard, I thought silly, even stupid, but I couldn't completely dismiss it, because at a deep level, due to my childhood, I realized it was a belief that I had embraced. I had to spend time digging down to find that truth, and I learned to mentally rehearse and prepare for a deliberate shift in my beliefs in order to change my behavior.

I challenge you to practice those four steps. Take twenty-one days to let go of an old belief and embrace a new one. Speak out loud the new belief. Speak it as truth. Say it in the present tense. Fix it in your logical mind and visual the feelings and behaviors you want for yourself. Deliberately connect those feelings and behaviors to the new truth. Maybe write that truth on a mirror where you see it each morning as you get ready for work. Or write it on an index card and keep it in your car. If you practice over a three-week period, you'll feel the old belief system fade. The ability to change your belief system will empower you with greater freedom and control, and that can feel like a life changing miracle.

Chapter 10

The Ladder of Inference

We constantly receive information through our five senses. In order to process that data, we compare it to paradigms we know, which leads us to make to certain assumptions about that information. As we process new data, we justify and refine our beliefs about the world through those assumptions, in other words, in light of previous examples. A reflexive loop forms in which we begin to see data only as it serves to reinforce our previous assumptions and paradigms. In business, as in life, it's important that our actions and decisions be grounded in reality. In the same way, when we accept or challenge other people's conclusions, we need to be confident that their reasoning is soundly based in fact. Emotional awareness allows us to challenge our assumptions so we can receive data with an open mind and process information in an unbiased way.

The ladder of inference, first put forth by organizational psychologist Chris Argyris and cited by Peter Senge in *The Fifth Discipline: The Art and Practice of the Learning Organization,* is a tool that can help you achieve sound reasoning. Sometimes known as the process of abstraction it's also useful for navigating difficult conversations. The ladder of inference illustrates the steps in your thinking that can lead you to jump to wrong conclusions, and so helps you stick to hard reality and facts. It lays out the mental steps from receiving data to drawing conclusions and explains how we adopt certain beliefs about the world. While our reasoning process feels logical, our analysis is always based on past experience, and everyone's experience is different.

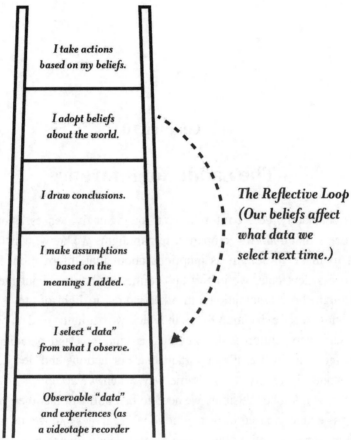

I take actions based on my beliefs.

I adopt beliefs about the world.

I draw conclusions.

I make assumptions based on the meanings I added.

I select "data" from what I observe.

Observable "data" and experiences (as a videotape recorder

The Reflective Loop (Our beliefs affect what data we select next time.)

Here's a summary of how the ladder of inference works, bottom up. At the bottom of the ladder is the pool of information available to us—observable data and experiences. At the next rung up, we select some of that information, typically whatever grabs our attention or seems particularly significant, and we ignore or filter out the rest. At the next step we make assumptions based on meanings we add by drawing from our personal and cultural understandings. We then draw conclusions based on those interpretations. At the top steps of the ladder, our conclusions inform our beliefs, which then drive our actions. A cycle of closed thinking has us refining and updating our beliefs about the world based on conclusions we've come to that are, in turn, based on assumptions we've made from our own experiences and cultural understandings. We can find ourselves in a closed loop or a bubble. Our belief systems are ultimately reinforced by what we choose to process, while our choices are influenced by our past experiences, which are different for each of us. None of us is on the exact same page, emotionally or intellectually. We choose the things that reinforce our own worldview and filter out those that challenge our worldview. This can lead to prejudice, intolerance, and a lack of empathy. It makes teamwork difficult and management a challenge.

Your beliefs might be founded on poor selection or faulty interpretation of data. For example, if you have a certain number of memorable interactions with a few clients or customers, you might generalize from those experiences and draw certain conclusions about the entire marketplace. Most of us follow mental steps that are subconscious, so we may be unaware of our assumptions. By using the ladder of inference as a reference tool, you can uncover the reasons for your reasoning, making you better at understanding yourself and your colleagues, so you can find the best solutions and overcome resistance to change.

In a difficult conversation, what you want to do is work your way back down the ladder. Someone has behaved—done or said something—in a certain way. Work your way down to the beliefs that led to that behavior, but don't stop there. *Why does one or both parties believe that? Where does that belief come from?* Ask for an example or a specific experience. *How was a particular conclusion reached? What assumptions led to that conclusion?* In a proper environment, you can collect puzzle pieces and deepen understanding as you work your way down the ladder of inference. It's a powerful tool for healing and strengthening relationships.

Chapter 11

Becoming a Person with High EQ

You have been learning EQ throughout your whole life, even though you may not have recognized it as such. Emotional intelligence not only *can* be learned, it *should* be learned. You are not born into the world with a predetermined capacity for emotional intelligence. The hard truth is, the only way to develop it is through practice. If you grew up in a family with high EQ, you probably started practicing your emotional intelligence at a young age, and the fact that EQ was modeled for you means you can train your kids in it as well. Think back to your teenage years. As you learned to relate to adults and your peers, there was presumably feedback from all quarters. You were complimented (told what you did well), criticized (told what you didn't do well), and through inclusion or seclusion, you discovered the specific ways you impacted others. Life itself gave you feedback. But did you always know how to use that feedback to improve and evolve?

> *Average players want to be left alone. Good players want to be coached. Great players want to be told the truth.*
> —*Doc Rivers*

No one is completely devoid of emotional intelligence. We all have it. The key is developing and strengthening it. One of the greatest training

grounds for developing emotional intelligence is interpersonal relationships. You don't strengthen EQ for the sake of strengthening it. You
want to further develop EQ in order to manage your reactions to those
around you so you can thrive in your relationships. There is a wealth of
useful, personal information to be gained through relationships if you
know how and where to look, data points that reveal who you are, what
you're good at, and what you're not. In the midst of any conflict there
are data points that reveal how well you regulate what is going on inside
you, but as any data analyst can tell you, personal information is useful
only to the degree that you know how to interpret and implement it.

Think about weight training. You work to build muscle by iso-
lating the muscle you want to strengthen. Once you've isolated the
targeted muscle, you begin a regimen of alternating exercise and rest.
You find an exercise that fully engages the muscle, and after a certain number of repetitions, you give it rest. You repeat the process of
engaging and resting until you reach a desired result. The longer and
more fully you engage the muscle, the stronger it gets.

The same principle applies to components of EQ. The more you
isolate a component of EQ and work to apply it in real-life relationships, the stronger that component becomes. The more you practice
the five components of EQ—social skills, empathy, self-motivation,
self-awareness, and self-regulation—by connecting with people on a
genuine level, the better you'll be at difficult conversations and the
stronger your EQ will grow, which will strengthen your relationships
and improve your life.

Life is as hard as it is wonderful. Relationships are the same. Being
teachable and humble enough to learn from experiences will help you
develop and grow your emotional intelligence. If you ever feel lost
regarding how to find your personal data points or effectively use that
information, ask yourself: *How do I process failure? How do I process
disappointment?* When you see your relationships or personal
motivation breaking down in specific areas, there is an opportunity to
grow your EQ. Some people ask me how long it takes to learn emotional intelligence. My answer may sound trite, but it's true nonetheless. You can learn to implement moments of EQ in a single day, but
success through continued growth is a lifelong process.

I'm proficient at many components of EQ. The feedback I get and my ability to process it is what has made my consulting practice so successful. Even so, I am constantly learning about myself. Every day I learn more about what others think of me and the impact I have on them. I process the things I do well and those I don't do well, particularly those things I don't do well. When I'm open to feedback and receive it well, I discover data points and pearls of wisdom that foster continued growth. I am able to train executive clients to heal and strengthen relationships through the process of difficult conversations. It is one of the things I am known for, but that doesn't mean difficult conversations are always easy for me. When I am in a difficult conversation and feel hurt or frustration, I follow the advice I give. I ask myself where my emotions are coming from. I examine my belief systems and choose to be honest about the areas where I'm weak or lacking. I commit to strengthening those areas through awareness and self-motivation.

EQ is sometimes a simple task. Other times it takes true bravery. Either way, emotional intelligence is essential to healthy relationships, which are at the heart of any thriving business or productive life. We are all still growing in emotional intelligence. The good news is, EQ is something that can be learned and developed. Your ability to manage yourself will make you successful working with others and a more effective leader. Developing your EQ will not only help you accomplish your goals, you'll be happier in the process.

Chapter 12

Emotional Intelligence and Leadership

Let's face it. If acquiring information were the only prerequisite for learning, anyone could pick up a dictionary, memorize its contents, and walk away with a pretty robust education. Intuitively, we know it takes more than that. But if the collection and memorization of raw data isn't true learning, what is? Real learning is the act of processing information to acquire and stimulate the formation of new ideas. No computer, as loaded with information as it may be, has ever come up with an original idea completely on its own. In other words, it's what you do with data that constitutes learning.

You might be reading this book on a mobile device, or maybe you consulted a search engine then surfed through tailored content on Amazon to find this book, or it may have popped up on your newsfeed because an algorithm used your personal search history to perceive your preferences and load customized ads aimed at your specific interests. We are all being custom scoped, segmented, and aggregated into information fields tailored to our supposed likes. Whether it's Google (a reference to *googol*, a large number meaning 10 to the 100th power), Bing (meant to connote the speed with which the world's information is available at our finger tips), or some other digital platform, evidence suggests we are truly living in an information age, or more aptly, an intelligence age. The question is—what kind of intelligence? Is intelligence really just the gathering, collection, and interpreting of facts? If so, then Siri and Alexa and the other devices that speak to our cars and thermostats and refrigerators and mobile devices are as smart as any of us. But do you really believe Siri or Alexa are good leaders? Or is there something missing from artificial intelligence, something that causes us to be more disconnected from true intelligence than ever before? We have more access to knowledge than any generation before, yet we seem to struggle more than ever with figuring out how to use it in real life situations to affect personal and societal change.

As we look ahead into the next century, leaders will be those who empower others. —*Bill Gates*

We are living in one of the most transformational times in hu- man history, replete with self-driving cars, quantum computing, and artificial intelligence. Science fiction has become science fact. The way we work has changed, and the skills we need are dramatically different than they were a generation ago. In a world where everything is connected, relationships become the coin of the realm. Emotional intelligence is more valuable than ever because it can't be digitized, automated by apps, or simulated by software. There has never been a greater need for empathy, social skills, and self-awareness.

After an exhaustive ten-year study, the Center for Creative Leadership, a think tank in North Carolina, came up with 67 attributes of effective leaders. Self-awareness was the highest ranked attribute. It makes sense. Leadership is about influence. If you are not in touch with the impact you have on others, how can you manage that impact in order to be successful in your leadership or management style? As a leader, you need to be aware of your influence on others. To be a positive influence on your team, you can't only be concerned with what you think or believe. You need to understand where the individuals on your team are coming from and the ways in which what you do or say impacts them. You can then be purposeful in how you lead. You can relate in ways that prove most effective for what your organization or team needs.

What's at stake is the future of leadership itself. The simple fact that we can learn the lessons of the past more easily than ever yet we seem more primed to repeat mistakes, shows a serious deficiency. If leadership at its core is all about influence—how to effect real change in people and environments in order to shape cultures at home, in business, and in society—then leaders need more than just the right data. They need to know how to put that data into play. Leaders need to know how to read the people they are leading. At the end of the day, management is about understanding the people right in front of you, not just what they are doing, but what is happening within them. Understanding and managing inner personal communication as well as interpersonal communication makes all the difference.

EQ in leadership is all too rare in this world of highly accessible IQ. Emotional intelligence in leadership is about managing hearts, emotions, and belief systems, as well as recognizing the obstacles people encounter while trying to learn knowledge and apply it with success. At the heart of emotional intelligence is the ability to help people and teams look inwardly and process what they find there. Stronger relationships, synergistic teams, and maximized productivity will result from leaders who are highly skilled at emotional intelligence. The transformation of knowledge into lasting learning and successful relationships takes time, but it is not out of reach. The first step is to acknowledge that information in a vacuum is insufficient.

John Haggai, author of the book *Lead on: Leadership That Endures in a Changing World,* gives a great definition of leadership. He says that leadership is the discipline of deliberately exerting special influence within a group to move it towards the goal of beneficial permanence that fulfills the group's real needs. In other words, a good leader knows what is helpful for the long term and can move a team toward that goal. A great leader can identify and clarify a group's true purpose and guide a team to achieve its goals. Since leadership is predominately about influence, a leader looking to grow will need to learn how to become better at positively influencing the people they lead. Despite what some believe, this doesn't always come naturally. For most, it's a learned skill.

All five components of emotional intelligence are critically connected to a leader's ability to lead. One way to increase your sphere of influence as a leader is to further develop your EQ. Leadership and influence are all about useful connections. The best way to influence others is through relationship. You may carry a leadership title and the authority that goes with it, but your influence is directly tied to how your team relates to you. Bulldozing them with angry commands and positional authority will not achieve beneficial permanence. You might get some things done in the short term, but you won't have a lasting effect.

It's difficult to lead with relational barriers in the way, and it's important to recognize that relational barriers are not limited to deep offenses. If you're simply too busy, unapproachable, or constantly distracted, your team may not feel the connection needed for success. On the other end of the spectrum, you might be overly involved. Perhaps you like to micromanage, feeling the need to mandate every detail of a project or goal. This can stifle creativity and engender a sense of mistrust. Any leader, if he is truly leading, will be consistently challenged by conflict and unforeseen roadblocks. A leader's ability to self-regulate can influence a team's success. Blow up at your team, and you'll distance yourself from the results you want. Drive people to burnout with unrealistic expectations or emotional instability, and you'll make it nearly impossible to repeat successes. You have to develop the ability to control your emotional responses to stress and conflict in order to keep a project going and set a positive example for those you are leading. Leadership is challenging. It's critical to establish and develop your own personal motivation.

> *Before you are a leader, success is all about growing yourself. When you become a leader, success is all about growing others.*   *—Jack Welch*

There is a book I often reference entitled *The Road Less Traveled*, by M. Scott Peck. In it, he writes about the proverbial crossroads of life—two paths in the forest. One path is the easy way, simple to navigate but not really leading where you want to go. The other road is filled with challenges and rough terrain, but it will bring you to exactly where you need to be. Getting a team to a place of beneficial permanence is difficult and rarely possible without resistance or pain. That's why developing emotional intelligence is so critical to becoming a good leader. Develop your sense of empathy, social skills, self-awareness, self-motivation, and self-regulation, set yourself up for effective teambuilding and sustained success, and embrace the road less traveled.

Chapter 13

Team EQ

All sorts of individuals form into teams: horses, fish, physicians, lawyers, scientists, soldiers, financial advisors, accountants, the list is almost endless. Pretty much anywhere you find individuals working or playing together, you'll find them forming into teams, because a group is stronger than an individual alone, and if the group can manage to operate as a single unit, it's more efficient as well. It's logical to assume the number of mates in a team will be a multiplier of how much stronger and more efficient that team will be compared to any individual member. Synergy increases ability exponentially, doesn't it? The truth is, five inept or uncoordinated people may be far inferior at an assigned task than one focused individual. There are teams that play or work like a single unit, like a well-oiled machine, but teams like that don't just fall together. They don't just happen. Great teams require strategic refinement and a whole lot of practice.

Chances are, at some point in your life you were part of a team. Most likely you still are, even if you don't view yourself that way. Sibling, spouse, business owner or employee, we're all part of the same team of human beings striving to survive and thrive. As it turns out, the very same EQ components that make you a better person, a more efficient worker, or a more effective leader can also be used to build a stronger team. As I said back at the beginning, it's all about relationships.

Social skills are about relating to others, the most crucial aspect of being on a team. On a team, you need to relate not only to individual teammates, but to the team as a whole. Your ability to communicate and relate to your team is critical to success. Suppose you were an amazing rower, asked to be part of a professional crew. As skilled and strong as you might be, if you were unable to row in unison with the rest of the team, your individual abilities wouldn't matter. Your inability to work with the rest of the crew would slow the entire team down and ruin its chances of success. The power of a team is found in how well it works as one. You still have to relate to each other as individuals, but also to the group as a whole. The team itself is a single organism, and sometimes what's best for an individual is not what's best for the team. A substitution or trade might be necessary. You may even have to take yourself out of the game for a bit for the sake of the team.

Likewise, when you consider team empathy, the principle is the same, but the method shifts from seeking to understand an individual to understanding the team as a whole. It's still important to listen to team members individually, but there comes a need to empathize with the collective perspective of the group. Individual points of view coalesce into a larger picture. Empathizing with an entire team of diverse perspectives allows individual voices to be heard and counted.

Team motivation, like individual motivation, requires a group to dig deep for inner strength, often in spite of setbacks, failures, or even plateaued successes. The benefit of team motivation is that you have people pushing you even as you push them, everyone collectively rallying emotional energy toward a shared goal. The potential downside is that, just as motivation can be contagious, discouragement or negativity can be as well. It only takes one naysayer to turn a group to the dark side. This is where the other components of team EQ come into play. Awareness of what is happening within a team can prevent a potential downward spiral.

When it comes to self-awareness as part of a team dynamic, you no longer seek mere individual awareness, but group awareness. You want to see beyond what each individual is doing to how each is affecting the other. You want to be aware of what is happening with the team as a whole. You're considering momentum and morale, looking for what might be hanging them up. Self-awareness translates directly to group awareness, which is crucial to any high performing team.

When a teammate starts to display negative or unhelpful behavior, the entire team is responsible for giving feedback. It's not just one person's responsibility or role to lead, coach, or correct. On a high performing team, the entire team responds and sends signals to let each other know what is helping or hindering. Mutual accountability unifies a team and helps drive momentum. Self-regulation becomes a group endeavor. It takes trust and time to achieve, of course, but group regulation is vital for any team's success.

> *There is no more powerful leadership tool than your own*
> *personal example.* —*John Wooden*

It's incredibly valuable to talk about the components of EQ with your teammates or the team you're coaching. In today's competitive business landscape, it's less about how skilled you are in a particular field, and more about your effectiveness in working with others. Relationships involving adaptability, social skills, empathy, person- al awareness, and regulation produce far better results for employers than any single artifice. The same is true for teams with a collectively high EQ. Sales teams, research teams, and executives all benefit from working well together. You might not be the leader of a team, but your role on that team is as important as anyone's. When you display a high level of emotional intelligence and model that behavior in the context of your team, you make yourself the most valuable kind of leader, one who leads by example.

PART TWO

The Art of Difficult Conversation

Chapter 14

The Cost and Rewards of Strengthening Relationships

Ninety percent of the clients I've interviewed in the course of my career say they were never provided a healthy model for dealing with conflict. In the house where I grew up, it was either fight or flight, blow up or shut up. Of course, neither of those models works well. Without a healthy, efficient model to emulate, navigating difficult conversations is even more problematic. One of the goals of this book is to provide insight into the process of difficult conversations and the use of tools for engaging in them successfully.

Years ago, I was hired to help an accounting firm that was part of a larger group of firms. Six partners had decided to split up. Three planned to stick together; the other three intended to splinter off and start their own firm. The network they belonged to warned them it would be expensive and difficult to break up in the way they were planning, but the partners felt it was their only option. I was brought in to facilitate the breakup. I interviewed all six partners. Each had strong feelings and complaints to share about one another. It was revealed that one of the partners had an anger management issue, prone to slamming doors and raising his voice. He was considered unprofessional at times. Two of the other partners supported him because he got a lot of work done and brought in a lot of revenue. The other three wanted no part of his antics. When I interviewed the three who were leaving, I asked if any of them had ever told the offending partner how they felt. They hadn't thought it necessary because the guy was slamming doors and yelling, so he obviously knew what he was doing and why they were upset.

I offered to teach them all some skills regarding how to have a difficult but constructive conversation. I suggested they put all their thoughts on the table before making a final decision to split up the firm. I initiated a group meeting where I offered some coaching and advice. They each described what they felt was working within the firm as well as what wasn't. Eventually, the partners were able to talk about things they'd never discussed together before. The one who had been slamming doors and losing his temper was the most surprised, even stunned by what was said about him. He had no idea the others were disturbed by his behavior. He'd just been venting frustrations and didn't realize his acting out was negatively impacting the business. He was embarrassed and a little ashamed. He apologized and promised to change.

The group conversation allowed them each to hear one another in a way they'd never done before. It was a powerful and productive meeting, after which they all decided to stick together and try to make things work without splitting up. I continued to work with them over an extended period. At the end of that time, things had changed dramatically. The offending partner was true to his commitment, adjusting his behavior and even seeking anger management counseling. The partners became more proactive about appreciating one other and about behaviors they deemed unacceptable. This allowed them to sit together and strategize, which enabled them to make decisions regarding the kind of firm they wanted to be and where they wanted to go as a business. Over the next few years, they made some pretty dramatic moves that resulted in their becoming a thriving firm with an impressive balance sheet, making more money together than they'd ever previously imagined. The point is, healthy conversation can drive change. When they came to me, they thought no amount of conversation could be helpful, but once they started talking about things they really needed to talk about, the conversation drove meaningful and productive change.

Difficult conversations are awkward & uncomfortable but necessary for strengthening & maintaining healthy relationships.

Difficult conversations are risky because they involve uncertainty. If you knew exactly where a conversation was going, what would be said and what would be decided, then it wouldn't be so hard. But you have no idea how it will end. The conversation could veer off somewhere you don't expect or don't like, someplace awkward and uncomfortable. Maybe your standing as a good neighbor will be ruined as a result of a conversation that doesn't go well. Perhaps as a parent you worry that a conversation will swerve into an argument that could destroy your relationship with your teenager. Your job might be affected by the outcome of a heated conversation. It might endanger your marriage. With every difficult conversation, you face the risk that a relationship will be strained to the point that it dramatically and negatively affects your life. I encourage you not to back away, but rather lean into those moments and proactively engage. Painful as it may be temporarily, that way leads to needed healing, productive change, and ultimately, personal and professional success.

Often the issue under discussion in a difficult conversation is not the fundamental problem that needs addressing. You think you know what the issue is, so you lean into it and you're really listening and suddenly you're around a corner you didn't see coming, surprised to find the topic is something you weren't prepared for, because the heart of the issue isn't the issue that started the conversation in the first place. You're a little lost and completely adrift. Difficult conversations can be scary as well as hard, but great risk brings great rewards.

Another reason difficult conversations are so trying is that it's uncomfortable to step outside one's own perspective or worldview, but remaining locked into a singular viewpoint makes it more likely a conversation will turn into a battle. It's important to realize different perspectives and learn from other points of view. If you're not good at that, or unwilling to even try, a difficult conversation becomes a war that you can only win by losing.

Effective conversation requires candor and courage, and that's always difficult. Most of us don't want to say anything that will hurt someone, just as we don't want to be hurt by words from others, so we avoid being too honest or going too deep. The problem is, it's of- ten necessary to dig deep in order to get to the core of an issue. That leaves us struggling with the delicate balance between candor and sensitivity. You don't want to say something that someone else is not going to like, but they need to hear it, and maybe you don't want to be forced to defend your words because you're not even sure if you can. Difficult conversations require you to be open and honest and brave, with yourself and with others.

The main reason a difficult conversation is so hard is that negative emotions are involved, and no one likes to experience bad feelings. Some choose the blow up or shut up route in order to avoid conflict altogether. Truth is, there are components to a difficult conversation that can make you feel bad in the moment even when you use a healthy process and ultimately achieve a productive outcome, but you can't allow fear of painful feelings to derail your desire for success in rela- tionships or in business.

Chapter 15

Two Types of Difficult Conversations

There are two types of difficult conversations, the ones you prepare for and the ones you are thrust into. Each has a different dynamic. Each requires a specific skill set. Sometimes difficult conversations arise without warning, with no time to prepare. You can't always predict when a difficult conversation will happen, so it's important to build a supply of appropriate responses for those times when you need them. Whenever possible, prepare your message to assure good communication.

I'm sure you've heard of *The Gettysburg Address*, but you may not have heard that President Lincoln wasn't the only speaker at the battlefield cemetery that day. In fact, he was discouraged from even attending because the organizers already had a professional speaker lined up. They gave Lincoln two minutes, and what he said in those 120 seconds were perhaps the most transformational and meaningful words ever spoken in so brief a time. Lincoln prepared, working tirelessly to get the language right. To this day we remember his speech, but who can recollect what the other professional speaker had to say that afternoon? Lincoln's preparation made all the difference.

In lesser events as well, preparation can be crucially important. Let's say you want a raise. You feel you deserve one and decide to ask your boss for it. So, you go to him and lay out your case for why a raise is justified, and let's say your boss agrees. He gives you the raise. You feel valued. It's a perfect outcome. But what if your boss doesn't agree, or for some other reason he just can't or won't authorize a raise? What do you do? Argue with him? Make demands? Quit? Maybe you feel devalued, unappreciated, not sure you even want to work for him anymore. But can you afford to lose the job? What is an acceptable outcome for this conversation? What do you really need? What might you be willing to settle for?

Now, let's say you're the boss. One of your employees comes to you asking for a raise. She makes a good case for herself, but your company is struggling, and the money isn't available at the moment. Do you explain the sensitive financial status of your business? Maybe she caught you at a bad time. She ambushed you in the parking garage after work. Do you say, *wish I could help, maybe later?* If she gets emotional or angry and starts to argue, do you fire her? If she quits, do you let her go, replace her with someone more grateful for the job? Maybe you'd like to keep her. Her coworkers respect her and perform better with her on the team. You've already invested time and energy in training her. How do you get her to stay without a raise? Make promises for the future? Offer alternate perks like a primo parking space or a longer vacation? What does this employee really need? What is she really asking for? Is it just money, or is she also hoping to be valued personally? Is she seeking encouragement, validation, understanding?

Years ago, a young man who was a line cook at a local restaurant came to me for coaching and advice. His life was out of balance because of his work situation. He was unhappy and wanted to talk to his boss, the restaurant owner, but he was unsure how to go about it. He felt undervalued and unappreciated. He wanted a raise or better hours as a sign that he was respected, but his boss was challenging to work for and just as difficult to converse with. So, I helped the young man outline exactly what he wanted to say, and we brainstormed all the ways his conversation with his boss might go—what she might say, how he should respond. While we were imagining various scenarios, he realized just how risky the conversation was going to be. More than anything, he was afraid of losing his job. I shared with him that I thought he might be worth more than he understood. An effective, caring, and conscientious cook is a valuable asset to any restaurant. I suggested, before having the difficult conversation with his boss, he should find out how much he was worth by applying for a few similar jobs elsewhere, just to determine the going rate and how sought after he might be. He filled out a couple applications, and sure enough, another restaurant in the area requested an interview then offered him a job. He asked for a little time to think about it, knowing he was now in a stronger position for that conversation with his boss. His boss, however, wasn't open to any of his input. She said she thought his salary was fine and that was the way it was and welcome to the restaurant business. He gave his two weeks' notice and took the other job. A month after he started at the new restaurant, the head chef quit and he was chosen to be the new head chef, with a substantial raise. Preparation had set the stage for what became an important turning point in his career.

A simple interaction like seeking a raise can quickly become a difficult conversation, fraught with potential pitfalls. The outcome could affect not only personal feelings on both sides but possibly the entire business model of the company. Winging it isn't a proper plan. You need to consider and prepare for potential emotions that might derail the conversation, insecurities that may have to be dealt with, other perspectives that might come into play. Be ready to manage your heart and marshal your thoughts by mentally preparing for possible eventualities. Formulate a script in your head, not just what you'll say but how you'll say it. Be careful about loaded words or phrases that will overstate your point or bring up other issues that might lead you into the weeds. Say the wrong thing, and you might offend your boss or your employee. A single wrong word can set off a touchy teenager. A wrong tone can cause your neighbor or your spouse to close off. Carefully choose the words, phrases, and tone that will be most helpful and effective.

Difficult conversations that are planned or expected allow time for preparation, but sometimes you're in one before you even know it. Back before my consulting practice became what it is today, I was co-owner of a store on the campus of The University of Illinois. We hired students to help run the store, and one day I was asked to lunch by one of the student managers. I knew her fairly well. She'd been on the middle school cross-country team I used to coach, and she'd grown into a fine young woman. I was delighted, thinking it would be an opportunity for us to catch up and share about life at the store, but things took an unexpected turn. All at once, she dumped on me. She was upset to put it mildly. She felt she'd been treated unfairly and accused me of helping create the unjust experiences and negative feelings that she was going through. Everything was somehow my fault. I'd been expecting a nice lunch and a friendly chat, but I found myself in a very difficult conversation.

You see, there'd been a robbery in the store some weeks earlier. Money had been taken from the safe, an inside job. The police interviewed her, as they had everyone connected with the store, but it seemed they were particularly suspicious of her. They'd questioned her over multiple interviews, blatantly insinuating that they believed she was the thief. They'd pressured her to come clean. "What did you do with the money?" they'd asked. Now she was near tears. Heightened by emotional pain and shame, her anger was palpable, and it was aimed at me. She saw everything as my fault. She felt I'd thrown her under the proverbial bus. She'd been blindsided, betrayed that I hadn't forewarned her. I was ill prepared for the conversation, because I had no idea what she'd been through. I knew she'd passed a polygraph test and the police had completely cleared her. I didn't know they'd ever been thinking of her as a suspect. In truth, I didn't know what the police had been thinking at all, and I should've been more aware. I should've offered to sit with her in the interview room or advised her to get legal counsel. We had a history together and she trusted me, which only heightened her feelings of betrayal.

I have to tell you, back then I didn't always do well when intense emotions were thrown my way. I tended to get defensive, which of-ten made matters worse, but that time I managed to listen as I tried to understand everything she was challenging me with. I didn't push back, didn't try to reason away or defend my position. The very act of sharing was helpful for her, and once her emotions were expressed, they dissipated. As pressure was released from the conversation, she suddenly stopped blaming and we were able to get through lunch. Later, I thought of all the things I should've said, so I went back to her and told her she was right and I was sorry. I reflected back to her all that I'd heard her say, and I let her know it was never my intention to sic the police on her. I respected her as a person and truly appreciated her work as a student manager. She continued working at the store until she graduated, and that experience actually brought us even closer. Difficult conversations often do.

When difficult conversations arise unexpectedly, it can be helpful to fall back on tried and true techniques. What follows is a six-step model that I developed through my consulting practice. It provides tools to help you manage your heart and navigate difficult conversations, especially during those times when you're forced to wing it. I urge you to memorize the model and practice the process until it becomes second nature.

Chapter 16

My Six-Step Model for Difficult Conversations

In the course of a difficult conversation, process is as important as any information that might be exchanged. Difficult conversations can be disorienting. My six-step guide can be used as both a toolbox and a road map. These six important touchstones can guide you through a healthy process.

Recognize the Problem

The first step is to recognize any strain in a relationship and acknowledge that a difficult conversation is needed. Awareness that something isn't right in a relationship and the commitment to pursue improving it are crucial. Suppressing emotions or avoiding conversation altogether may seem like an appropriate response but it will result in broken relationships. It is not a sign of weakness to admit when there is a problem—it is a sign of strength. If there is a strain in your relationship, if something needs clarification or maybe you just feel something's not right, it's important to recognize that a difficult conversation is needed. Be self-aware and proactive. The sooner you get into a healthy process, the greater your chances of successfully repairing a relationship.

The most common method of dealing with relationship problems is the model I learned as a boy from my four older brothers. Blow up or shut up. The Chisholms were a clan that tended to hold back. Whenever possible, we avoided conflict. Unwilling to process our pain together, we shut up or shut down. We didn't generally talk about emotional turmoil or personal problems until things boiled over or exploded, in other words, until there was an obvious mess to clean up. I remember a few screaming matches. Now and then an argument was settled with fisticuffs. Whoever had the authority or the bigger fists usually won out in the end. As the runt of the family, that wasn't a viable option for me.

The truth is, blowing up only further strains a relationship, undermining the ability to work together effectively. Shutting up or shutting down has the same effect. It just takes a while longer. You can avoid confrontation in the short-term, but heart issues will only build, become stronger, and bite you even more on your long-term backside. The good news is, with guided practice and experience, it's possible to get better at difficult conversations, and relationships grow stronger when you do. It has been a long journey, but my siblings and I somehow survived, and we're closer now than ever.

So, first step: Realize and recognize when there is a problem. If you want to be good at relationships, if you want to be good at life, you have to be in touch with your own feelings and attuned to the feelings of others, which underscores the importance of developing your emotional intelligence. Then you can be proactive about addressing the problems that cause strain in your relationships.

Choose Appropriately

The next step, if possible, is to choose an appropriate time and place as well as the appropriate participants for your difficult conversation. You also need to appropriately frame the relationship that is at risk so you can effectively chart the conversation.

Too often, people approach a difficult conversation thinking to get in and out as quickly as possible because it's uncomfortable, or else they're focused on winning, which means someone is going to lose. Relationships are why life exists, so be careful about a win-lose mindset. If all you're concerned about is winning, you're going to choose a time and place suited to that outcome, but if you're trying to strengthen a relationship, you'll choose differently. Difficult conversations, if not framed well, won't end well. If you frame the conversation as an argument, and you're successful, well, the good news is, you won the argument. The bad news is, you may have destroyed a relationship and perhaps even the ability to work with the other party.

Remember, it's the relationship that you're fighting for, not victory in the argument. Your mindset shouldn't be about securing a win. The purpose of a difficult conversation is to strengthen a relationship, though it doesn't always feel that way. Sometimes it feels more like a contest, one you don't want to lose. Still, it's important not to be adversarial. Whether you're trying to understand and strengthen an intimate relationship like a marriage or one with your child, or it's a more impersonal relationship with a teammate or a business partner, maybe even a simple conflict with a neighbor who you don't have much of a relationship with at all, whatever the state of that relationship, you need to properly frame it so you can use the difficult conversation to build from there. Knowing your purpose is empowering. It's also helpful to a healthy process.

The right time for a difficult conversation is rarely when the conversation pops up. Friday evening at 5:30 is probably not the best time to start a difficult conversation with a coworker. Neither is Monday morning at 7:30. So, when is the right time? Lunch? After a staff meeting? When should you broach a difficult subject with your spouse? Just before bed? After dinner? In front of the Tv? In front of the kids? Should you confront your neighbor a week after he blocked your driveway with his garbage cans, or right now while he's mowing his lawn? Try to choose an appropriate time that allows all involved to fully participate.

The best location for a difficult conversation is one where it's possible to create a safe environment so all parties can be candid with one another. Don't corner someone in a dank basement or in a room full of distractions. If possible, choose a place where all parties are comfortable and on an even footing, not on one party's home turf and certainly not in an all glass conference room where passersby can observe.

If a difficult conversation is going to be truly effective, it's also important that all the right people participate. Who needs be involved? Just the two of you? Are there others with important input? It's sometimes wise to consider a third party to facilitate, someone to help foster a safe environment that allows effective and candid conversation.

In a difficult conversation, when possible, choose an appropriate time, an appropriate place, and the appropriate participants, and remember to appropriately frame the relationship that is at risk so you can strengthen and improve it.

Collect Puzzle Pieces

Step three is to collect puzzle pieces and bring them out into the open. As a management consultant I'm often hired to facilitate difficult conversations when a situation has become untenable. While interviewing key participants, I'm often told the problem is unfixable. I quickly discover there are aspects to the relationship at risk that are hidden beneath the surface or simply misunderstood by one or more parties. The situation is only unfixable as long as important information is missing or obscured. Solving the puzzle of relationship problems requires all the pieces. In my experience, healthy process helps get puzzle pieces on the table. The unfixable becomes fixable when all the pieces of the puzzle are present. You have to consider everyone's perspectives, their experiences and thoughts, and you need to make room for emotions, theirs as well as yours.

> *You are a piece of the puzzle of someone else's life. You may never know where you fit, but others will fill the holes in their lives with pieces of you.*   —Bonnie Arbor

Making room for uncomfortable ideas and feelings isn't easy. It can be painful to hear what others are feeling and thinking about you. You have to set your heart in a proper posture in order to collect puzzle pieces. You have to be willing to hear what someone else is thinking, even if you disagree. That's how puzzle pieces are collected. You have to be attuned to what others are thinking and what they're feeling. You have to consider factors that may be contributing to the strain in the relationship, and you must be willing to share what you're thinking and feeling, what you see as contributing factors. The better you get at collecting puzzle pieces, the better you'll be at solving problems and healing relationships, and you'll be better at both if you're committed to working at it.

Keep in mind, often the issue is not the issue. You're thinking a difficult conversation is about an event that happened last Tuesday, but as you start collecting puzzle pieces, you find it's connected to something that happened six months ago. It may be connected to things you didn't know were connected at all, because you didn't understand all of the dynamics. At the heart of most relationship problems is unhealthy process. Become proficient at collecting puzzle pieces. The better you get, the better you'll be at solving the issues that drive difficult conversations.

Manage P.I.E.

Step four is to manage P.I.E., and no, that's not Thanksgiving menu advice. It's an acronym for the three major problems that usually hang up or derail difficult conversations. First is the issue of **perspective**— the P in P.I.E. In difficult conversations, perspective can be a sticky wicket. It's hard enough to step outside one's own perspective. It's even more difficult to make room for others'. Two people may think they're confronting the same issue, experiencing the same thing, when they're not. It's important to get outside your own perspective and make room for the other person's take on the issues at hand. That's what I mean by managing perspective.

As you approach a difficult conversation, your thought process will include knowing what you've experienced and what you're feeling. You know what the issue is. The issue is the other guy. You've already reached that conclusion. That's your perspective, but if you lead with that, you're basically done already. You're not going to do a very good job of collecting puzzle pieces. Step outside your own understanding and make room for the other person's point of view. Take a heart posture that says, *there are things I'm going to learn from this conversation. I don't have the whole truth and nothing but the truth. I have a perspective, and that's all it is, so it's okay if it gets challenged.*

We don't all have the same worldview. Your perspective may be radically different from others. That's okay. It's just a perspective, one of many, and the better you are at stepping outside yours, the healthier you'll be in relating to others. Two people can experience what seems to be a single event, but actually, it's not the same for each because it is filtered through different belief systems and separate points of view, the unique lenses through which each individual looks at life. In a difficult conversation, with a relationship at stake, you have to share your experiences, what is important to you, what has impacted you, and at the same time realize that your point of view will be different from that of the other person. Recognizing and accepting that truth becomes important when collecting puzzle pieces. You need to manage perspectives. Learn how to step outside your own experience and make room for a different point of view.

The I in P.I.E. stands for **insecurities**. In difficult conversations, it's common to feel at risk. Something may happen that could set you off, which could hurt your career, which could hurt your marriage or your relationship with your children. Learning to manage insecurities is crucial. I'm often reminded of the time I spent coaching one of the owners of a prominent construction company, a man with a remarkably strong personality. He supervised his business with an iron fist and experienced a great deal of success, but he had a hard time with difficult or strategic conversations. We were making headway regarding his personal growth. Some really good things were happening with his business, and we decided to work on leadership development. He was one of a group of partners who owned the company, so I devised a plan requiring all of the owners to address leadership qualities in their lives. Along with a battery of other tests, I had them take intelligence tests.

On the day that I brought in the test results, my client with the strong personality was unusually nervous, as though he expected poor results. He seemed almost scared, which was very uncharacteristic for him. He was mostly worried about the intelligence tests, and I came to understand that he was nervous because he had done so poorly in school when he was growing up. He saw himself as stupid. In fact, he'd been told he was stupid too many times. As I began to go over his test results with him, he already knew his score would be below average. What the test actually showed was that he was very bright. It also revealed that he had a learning disability. This accomplished man in his late fifties never knew he had a learning disability that made traditional schooling more difficult for him. When I told him the test actually revealed he was quite bright, tears filled his eyes. I think we both understood that much of his personal strength was a counterbalance, a way to make sure that nobody ever saw that he was stupid. His insecurity had become a driver in his life, one that he'd used effectively, but once that puzzle piece was laid on the table, he was able to begin creating a new image of himself.

We all have tender spots, places in our lives, in our hearts, where we feel vulnerable, where we are not completely confident. Maybe you have issues of brokenness or traumatic memories. Difficult conversations can threaten to expose those insecurities. Another person might even try to use your vulnerabilities and insecurities against you in an effort to win an argument. That is poor process and a sure recipe for the destruction of a relationship. Learn to make room for insecurities, yours and others', and never use anyone's vulnerabilities as a weapon. If your insecurities are being pinched, stop the conversation for a minute. Don't avoid the conversation or just walk away. Don't make a fight-or-flight decision while your insecurities are under attack. Take a time-out. Compose yourself. And be careful not to shoot the messenger. Follow up after a difficult conversation to focus on why you were feeling a certain way. Allow healing. Consider what happened inside you, your thoughts and feelings. Something said, something laid on the table threw you off, caused you pain. Why? There are skills and tools I'll share with you that can help, but the main thing is to understand the tender issues in your own heart that may rise up and spill over during a difficult conversation. Learn to manage your insecurities so you can stay engaged in the conversation and not be derailed by them.

Lastly, the E in P.I.E stands for **emotions**. Often the heart of a difficult conversation is not a single topic. It's a cauldron of emotions. Learning how to make room for emotions without letting them take over or derail the conversation, without blowing up or causing the other side to do the same, can be the difference between success or failure. Some pointed thing may be said that hurts or sets you off. That will happen sometimes. Instead of responding from that place of hurt or anger, take a timeout so you can manage your insecurities. You don't want emotion to direct the conversation or control how effective you can be at collecting puzzle pieces.

Emotions want to take on a life of their own in difficult conversations. They are a part of how we process life. In fact, that's their purpose. When bad things happen, sadness helps us process those things. When we're indignant, it's anger that helps us process what has happened to us. Let me reiterate an important truth—it's not what happens to you that causes your emotions. It's what you believe about what happens to you that causes your emotions. Think about it. If something that happens causes you to be emotional, then that means your emotions are out of your control, because you can't control what happens to you. You can only control how you respond to it. There is power in that insight.

Difficult conversations are usually influenced by out of control emotions.

Emotions may be unavoidable in a difficult conversation. If you understand where your emotions are coming from, those emotions will help you process events. Do you remember that movie about no crying in baseball? Some think there's no crying in business. Of course, they're wrong. Relationships are at the core of all business, and difficult conversations are a means of strengthening those relationships. Difficult conversations may sometimes stir emotions that can and should be processed. If you're discussing important topics that could affect your career, it will probably get emotional. Be aware and make room for that. Remember, expressed emotion dissipates. Unexpressed emotion may build to the point of explosion, which can derail a conversation or a career. Don't let your emotions lead the way. Make room for them and affirm them, but manage them. You won't be successful in business or personal relationships if you hold back or avoid difficult conversations just because you fear they may be too uncomfortable or painful. If you don't manage your emotions, you might blow up and vomit them into the conversation. Realize that emotions are an important and acceptable part of the process, and although you can't control everything that happens to you, you can control your responses.

So, that's step four—manage P.I.E., perspectives, insecurities, and emotions, the three major issues that derail most difficult conversations.

Stay on Track

Step five is a reminder of how important process is. In a difficult conversation, it's easy to get off track. Sometimes, you become so focused on the content of a conversation that you lose sight of its process. All of a sudden, you're talking about six things instead of one. Things get heated and emotions take over. Keep asking yourself the refocusing questions: *What are you trying to accomplish? Is there a better way to do it? Are you really listening? Are you effectively collecting puzzle pieces? Do you feel heard? Are you feeling hurt? Do you need to call a time-out? Are you in healthy process? Are you on track? Are you following the steps of the model?* Be direct, specific, and honest. Don't talk around what you're trying to say. Speak with kind, direct language that specifically states where you're coming from and the goal you're trying to achieve in order to make sure the conversation stays on track.

Come to Closure with Consensus & Accountability

The final step in the six-step model is to properly negotiate closure, which necessitates consensus and accountability. Your goal should not be to just get through a difficult conversation. You should be trying to move a relationship forward. Remember, it's the relationship you are fighting for, not victory in the argument. At the end of the conversation, what have you agreed to, and how do you make sure there is accountability regarding what has been agreed upon? What will be different as you move forward?

> *There will come a time when you believe everything is finished. That will be the beginning.* —Louis L'Amour

Too often in a difficult conversation, parties reach a breakthrough and everyone feels better. They think, great, we finally made it to a good place. They're tempted to stop there. But it's not truly over until a consensus is reached regarding what's been resolved. What exactly has been agreed to? What is expected going forward? What if one party doesn't follow through? How will all parties be held accountable? Those issues must be addressed in order to reach complete resolution. The best time to talk about accountability is not after somebody has broken the agreement. Discuss what accountability might look like and come to an agreement about that. Relationships require tending. It's necessary to check in and follow through after a difficult conversation because fruitfulness may only bear out over time.

Also, and this is important, remember that apologies and forgiveness are key aspects of closure. The words, "I'm sorry" and "I forgive you" are powerful. They can heal and change everything.

Effective closure and appropriate follow-through after a difficult conversation empowers a healthy process moving forward. In that way, a difficult conversation becomes a springboard to a stronger relationship.

Chapter 17

The Power of Listening

When you have no time to prepare for a difficult conversation because it's arrived unexpectedly, one thing you can do is slow it down. The tendency is to get in and out of a difficult conversation quickly because it doesn't feel good, it's risky, and you're unprepared. Emotions intensify and mistakes are made. Pieces are missed and things blow up. If you find yourself thrust into a difficult conversation, it's best to slow things down and give yourself time to work up appropriate responses. The most powerful way to slow down a difficult conversation is to be an effective listener. Listening skills can help slow a conversation and keep it from sliding off the rails. You can slow the pace and buy time for clearer thinking simply by acknowledging or affirming with phrases like: *I hear you saying...* or *I sense you're feeling...* If the other person isn't listening well, you might say, *Wait a minute, before you respond, what did you hear me say?* or *What do you think I'm feeling right now?* That will provide extra time to keep managing and processing your thoughts, allowing you to get out ahead of them and prepare.

Have you ever been trained in how to collect your thoughts and present them in written form? That would be a composition class, and you probably took one as early as grade school. Have you ever taken a class on how to gather your thoughts and present them orally? That would be a speech class. Many in business and in the arts have taken such courses. But have you ever taken a class or been trained in how to listen? Probably not. It's not unusual to have some training in how to compose or present a point of view, but when everyone is sharing and nobody is listening, effective communication fails. You have two ears and one mouth. To be effective in difficult conversations, you should do twice as much listening as speaking. Though most have not been trained in it, listening is a skill that can be learned and improved.

Most people do not listen with the intent to understand; they listen with the intent to reply.   *—Steven Covey*

One of the sincerest forms of respect is listening to what someone has to say. To spend time seeking to understand what someone is saying is an investment, a deposit into a relationship. Too often, while one is talking, the other is preparing a response instead of investing the energy it takes to truly understand what's being revealed. The heart of effective communication is the give and take of speaking and listening that creates an effective environment for collecting puzzle pieces. It's been said you should speak in such a way that others will love to listen to you and listen in a way that others will love to speak to you. It's important to gather and listen for information that others are sharing, and just as important to honor that information in a way that makes room for healthy dialogue. The three components of effective listening are: Ears, Eyes, and Heart.

Listening Ears

For some, listening is a period of impatient waiting until they get   a turn to attack. They wait for the speaker to take a breath so they can unload their word ammunition. Don't be one of those people. Listening should be a genuine effort to understand what someone else is saying, and to do so without prejudging. It takes focus and a willingness to spend time and energy to truly comprehend what's being said. I repeat—not just hearing what's said, but also understanding it.

Your brain can go a lot faster than your ability to speak, even faster than your ability to listen, so be careful not to spend too much energy framing your argument when you should be focused on what the other party is sharing. As you listen to their words, also consider the tone being used. There's a lot of information there. Tone is a part of conversation and can change the message, so be aware of it.

Also, listen to feedback without getting defensive. If you find yourself with your hackles up, ask yourself why? Try paraphrasing or reflecting back at the speaker the feedback you're hearing to be sure you're understanding correctly. If you automatically get defensive, you'll stop listening. Remember, all feedback is good because it gives you valuable information. The better you get at receiving feedback, the more of it you will get. If you shoot the messenger, you won't get any more messages. The posture with which you receive allows you to receive more. Even if you don't always agree with it, you need feedback to help you grow. It's great insight into what someone else sees and what their perspective is.

Approach any difficult conversation with humility and openness, but do not blindly accept feedback as truth. Let it in and give yourself time to think about it. Weigh what's being said and avoid the two extremes—fully receiving it or outright rejecting it immediately. Paraphrase the feedback to be sure you really understand what the other person is sharing. Make sure your understanding is correct. If you feel something is off about what you are hearing, perhaps it's because the person giving the feedback has a blind spot that you are picking up on. Or maybe you're the one with a blind spot. There's no short cut. You have to focus on the task at hand—listening.

Listening Eyes

Your ears aren't your only tool for listening. You can listen with your eyes as well. Just as important as the words being shared is the data being transmitted through body language. If the other person's arms are crossed, if they seem distant, if they're not making eye contact, they're probably disconnected. Reading body language is an important component of listening. Notice the other person's eyes and facial expression. Are they fidgeting? Are they uncomfortable? Those are important data points for you. Read their signals to pick up important information that may be essential to a healthy process for effective conversation. How much attention is the other party giving you as you speak? You may need to call that out. Without anger, you might say, *I understand you have a lot going on. You're looking at your phone as I'm talking. Do me a favor? Could you put that down? I think this conversation is really important.*

Body language speaks. Listen with your eyes. Many times, while I'm facilitating a conversation between two parties in a business setting, someone will say something and I'll see someone else's eyes roll or glaze over. That's a signal of an emotional response. They're controlling it, but their eyes give them away. It's a tell, and it's an opportunity for me to ask what's behind the reaction I just noticed.

In order to effectively listen, you have to adopt the mindset that every person can teach you something. You might not always agree with what's being said, but to know and be known is the true mark of effective communication. By taking time to listen to what others are saying, you are conceding that their thoughts deserve consideration. You are acknowledging their worth as a fellow human being, and you're also more likely to be listened to in exchange.

Of course, you need to look out for your own body language as well. Communication begins before you utter your first word. Nonverbal communication through your gestures and facial expressions provides a first impression. It's been over forty years since author and management consultant Gerard Egan introduced his five steps of attentive listening. Known by the acronym SOLER, it is an aid for teaching and learning about nonverbal communication and can be a powerful tool in any difficult conversation.

S—Square up. Demonstrate your interest and engagement by posturing yourself appropriately. Face the person you are communicating with. You want to send a message that you're interested.

O—Open up. Refrain from crossing your legs or folding your arms across your chest, and never clench your fists. You don't want to convey aggression. Keep an open posture to indicate your openness to what the other person is saying.

L—Lean in. Simply leaning towards the other person shows you are involved and makes them feel they are being heard and understood.

E—Eye contact. Maintaining eye contact shows interest and concern; however, it's important to vary eye contact so the other party doesn't feel threatened or intimidated. You don't want to get into a stare down, but neither do you want to avoid eye contact altogether. You want to connect.

R—Relax. It's important to stay calm and avoid fidgeting when another person is talking. Don't pace or twirl the ring on your finger. Conveying calm to the other person will help them relax.

Listen with your ears, but listen also with your eyes. As you focus and look for cues, you may be surprised how much data you can gain to help you navigate a difficult conversation.

Listening Heart

Listening with your ears and eyes is important, but perhaps the most influential aspect of effective listening is your heart posture, which involves seeking to understand the other side even when you disagree, even if what the other party says hurts or offends you. A right heart posture says: *Because I want to understand, I'm willing to make room for you. I'm interested in what you're thinking and what you're feeling, so I'm going to invest, focus, and apply my energies toward strengthening this relationship.* It's not easy, and it definitely takes commitment.

Antoine de Saint-Exupéry was onto something when he recognized that it is only with the heart that one can see rightly; what is essential is invisible to the eye. Heart posture is the hardest part of effective listening. It takes heart to sustain focus and energy, even when you don't like it, even when it doesn't feel good and it's risky and a little bit scary. It's a challenge to remain fully engaged and fully present in a difficult conversation, though the results can be powerfully transformative. Listening with your heart allows you to truly understand a relationship and improve it. It takes practice and commitment to train your heart to seek understanding and deliberately pursue it, but once acquired, it can become a habit that will strengthen your relationships, improve your business, and enrich your whole life.

Chapter 18

Reflective Listening

One of the best tools for effective listening is reflective listening. It's based on the EQ component of empathy, which is the act of understanding, being aware of, being sensitive to, and vicariously experiencing the feelings, thoughts, or experience of another. Because effective listening seeks to understand, it is helpful at times to use reflective listening. Reflective here is meant as in a mirror, not as in deeply thoughtful. It's a method of paraphrasing and repeating back a message you've received to be sure it's the same message that was sent. It may surprise you how often that's not the case. Sometimes you understand exactly what someone else is trying to say, but often there are barriers to effective communication. You may use certain words that mean specific things to you while they may mean something different to someone else. Others may have a different education or socioeconomic background. Their different life experiences or their vocabulary or expressive abilities may create barriers to effective communication, making a difficult conversation even more difficult. In such instances, reflective listening can break down walls.

First, you need to determine whether reflective listening is even necessary. Someone might come running into the room and frantically ask, *where's the bathroom?* If you're practicing your reflective listening skills, you might respond, *I sense that you're a little frustrated because you don't know where the bathroom is.* But that's the wrong time for reflective listening. Somebody just needs to know where the bathroom is. Not every communication requires you to kick into reflective mode. However, in a difficult conversation, when you're trying to understand but don't get what the other person is trying to say, reflective listening can be a useful tool. So, first assess. Is it the time for reflective listening?

Next, you want to identify the emotions being expressed and the thoughts behind those emotions. Maybe the other party is frustrated because of an event that happened between the two of you last week. You might need to tentatively reflect back, *I think I hear you saying that you're frustrated because of last Tuesday's event. Am I hearing you correctly?* The other party might say, *yes, that's what I said and that's what I meant.* Terrific. You have understanding. But the other person might say, *no, that's not the point I'm trying to make. I'm not frustrated. I'm angry.* Or, *I'm not frustrated. I'm sad.* It may be necessary to clarify, to make sure the message that the other person is trying to communicate is the one you're receiving, and vice versa. Seek first to understand before being understood, but periodically clarify your own words, make sure what you're sharing is getting across. Ask that your feelings and thoughts be reflected back to you. Obviously, this slows the conversation down, but it can ultimately save time to weigh in with each other. When your brain is churning, you'll want to respond to what was said without checking whether you heard it right. The other person's brain is churning too, and the conversation goes fast. You talk, they talk, you talk, they talk. You may have disconnected three exchanges ago, and now you're far along in the conversation and suddenly something blows up, because you never really heard one another back there.

Reflective listening forces you to break a difficult conversation into manageable chunks, so one party doesn't share for twenty minutes straight without checking in, making it hard for the other party to keep up or remember all the responses they wanted to give. Reflective listening is effective listening. Reflect back to the other person what you are hearing. *This is what I hear you saying. You're feeling this because of this. Am I hearing you correctly?* Build on that. Allow the other person to reflect back to you in the same way. It's not hard to fall into a rhythm, each of you taking a turn going back and forth. That's effective communication, and that's what you want in a difficult conversation. Reflective questions should be tentative, not authoritative, not, *this is what you're saying,* but rather, *I think this is what you're saying. Is that right?*

The authority on any message being delivered is the one delivering it, the one with a message to communicate. The other party is momentarily weighing in to make sure the message received is the one that was sent. One is the authority; the other is tentatively verifying, until their roles reverse. Be careful about getting into a parental mode with the person or team you are speaking with. Be nonpunitive in your communication. Anything that enables or encourages shame will cut off effective learning. You want to help by speaking to a blind spot and not make it more difficult to see because of the punishing style of your communication.

Remember, the goal of reflective listening is not to move the conversation in a specific direction but simply to understand the person you're talking to. So, determine whether the situation calls for reflective listening. Identify the thoughts and feelings being expressed, then tentatively summarize and reflect them back to the speaker. Reflective listening isn't only for collecting puzzle pieces. The fact is, some folks don't even know what they are thinking or feeling. If you do a good job of reflective listening, you can help them clarify their thoughts and define the emotions driving them, which ultimately benefits you both. It's a powerful tool that can bring clarity to a difficult conversation.

Curiosity, Concision, & Affirmation

It can be transformative to engage in wholehearted listening while creating a safe environment to collect puzzle pieces, so let me offer you three more useful skills that relate to effective communication. The first involves the art of **curiosity**. You share, and I reflect back to you my understanding, and it's obvious we are hearing each other. We're doing a decent job of communicating, but we don't want to just

echo each other. We want to understand one another. It may take a
little probing to reach a deeper understanding. Perhaps I use a particular word that troubles or confuses you. Maybe it causes an emotional
response in you. You might ask what that word means to me or why I
used it. You might need to inquire about what's being shared in order
to delve deeper. Don't be afraid to ask, but tread lightly. Make it clear
your purpose is to better understand. It's possible to ask questions in
such a way that you shut the other person down. That's unproductive
and not what you want to do. You want to ask questions that draw the
other person out, not shut them up. That's the artful part of curiosity.
You want to ask questions that bring puzzle pieces onto the table. *Why
do you think that? When did you start feeling that way? Can you give
me another of example of the point you're making? Can you help me
understand what you're getting at?* When collecting puzzle pieces in
order to strengthen a relationship, it's sometimes necessary to inquire
about the other person's thought process or feelings or experience.
Remain curious, even if you believe you have the other person figured
out. Difficult conversations can take unusual turns.

A difficult communication skill to master, but one that can help
strengthen relationships by facilitating difficult conversation, is
concision—using few words to convey much meaning, getting to the
point and keeping to the point. You don't want just to tell what you're
thinking and feeling. You want to help someone understand why
you're thinking and feeling that way, so you pour out your thoughts as
well as the reasoning behind them, sometimes with swirling emotions
tangling your tongue. If it's a difficult conversation for which you've
had time to prepare or rehearse, if only in your mind, it will likely be
a bit easier, but problems arise when your brain is racing, fueled by
emotion, and you're not sure yourself what your thoughts are until you
think them, and you're not comfortable with how you're feeling or why.
You're trying to state your case, defend your arguments, trying to
convince the other party that you know what you're saying and what
you're saying is right. If it takes you an hour to make a single point, a
difficult conversation will be even more difficult and less effective.
The quicker and more pointed you can be about what you're thinking,
why you're thinking it, what you're feeling and why you're feeling it,

the more likely you'll stay on track, and the more effective you'll be. To do that, it's best to share your reasoning by using concrete examples without difficult or inflammatory words. The other party is trying to process along with you. Avoid the confusion caused by rambling or getting sidetracked. Get to the point, be clear and concise, and stick to the point. Concision is an effective communication skill that can make difficult conversations more bearable.

Another important component of reflective listening, as well as a useful tool for effectively navigating a difficult conversation, is **affirmation**. Even if you don't like what you're hearing, it's important to affirm what the other party is sharing. That's healthy process. You're working to strengthen a relationship through difficult conversation because that relationship is important, and it's powerfully productive to be good at relationships. In a difficult conversation, when you don't like or agree with what you're hearing, it's even more necessary and important to create a safe space for both parties. Don't forget, the other party is collecting puzzle pieces, too. You want to outwardly affirm even as you inwardly disagree, because the relationship is what's most important. *I appreciate you. I appreciate what you just shared. I understand how important this topic is to you. I admire the commitment you make to this organization, to this team. Even though we disagree, I respect you. I appreciate a particular thing about you, something in your personality or your work or your effort.* Look for opportunities to affirm. Acknowledge emotions, perspective, history, and diversity. People who are good at affirmation are able to draw others out even as they disagree. It's a powerful tool. Get that working for you and your success at creating an environment for collecting puzzle pieces will dramatically increase.

The artful skills of curiosity, affirmation, and concision, in combination with reflective listening, can build an incredibly effective communication environment in which puzzle pieces are laid on the table, allowing difficult conversations to be truly effective. The entire process builds empathy, thereby increasing emotional intelligence, which is pivotal to healthy relationships in the workplace and at home.

Chapter 19

Tentativeness

You've probably picked up on the fact that the five components of EQ—self-awareness, self-regulation, self-motivation, empathy, and social skills—are all utilized in difficult conversations. In fact, they are even strengthened through the process. Leaning into difficult conversations helps develop muscles needed to strengthen EQ and to be an effective leader, but it's unhelpful to boldly declare yourself without giving consideration to the other party. Confident declarations may win arguments but they don't invite conversation. What is needed to be successful in a difficult conversation is language that makes room for others' thoughts and ideas. If you show up in a conversation declaring, *this is the way it is. I've achieved a lot of success in my life, so I'm sure about my thoughts because that's where my success has come from, and I believe what I believe, and that's the way it is*, then you're forcing the other party to be confrontational, to take you on in order to get a different point across. That's not healthy process and no way to create a proper environment for revealing and collecting puzzle pieces.

Being tentative as you express ideas is a crucial skill for effectiveness in a difficult conversation. Tentative language invites participation. It's a skill that can and should be learned. It sounds like this: *I'm not exactly sure, but I think this is a major contributing factor, and I want to know what you think. I've been wrestling with this, and I'm not sure whether to share it, but I'm thinking this could be important.* You might be certain in your mind or your heart that your ideas are correct, that you understand a deeper truth, but without tentativeness, you'll close off opportunity and undercut the other person's ability to fully participate.

I once had a client who was a strong-willed man, not particularly self-aware, focused mostly on what was important to him. He often bulldozed people with his opinions. Effective, strategic planning requires everyone involved to have a voice in the conversation, so I felt I needed to make the point to him that the way he was running his life was working against his stated goals. At one point, during a strategy retreat at a resort hotel, I asked this client to join me in the bar. There I told him that the way he was leading his life was counterproductive. The look on his face told me he didn't understand. I said to him, "Who you are at work has everything to do with who you are in life." I then asked him to dance with me. He was confused, so I grabbed his hand and pulled him up out of his chair. I told him I wanted to show him something. We were in a public setting and it was a bit embarrassing for us both, him especially because he didn't understand what I was trying to illustrate. I proceeded to march him around the seating area next to the bar, not just leading, but gripping and pushing and shoving him. After a brief but rough turn around the makeshift dance floor, I pushed him back into his chair. He was more than a little upset and demanded to know what I thought I was doing. "That's what it's like for others to dance with you," I said. Then I told him I wanted to show him what it could be like, what it should be like. I encouraged him to stand again. I placed my hand on his shoulder, and slowly we moved together around the room. Weird as it was, he was red faced with embarrassment, but he smiled. Everyone in the bar was watching as I gently led him back to his chair. When we were seated again, I said, "Leadership isn't only about knowing where to go. It's about how to get people there by working with them, not pushing through them or over them or dictating to them. You need to make a change, from one type of dancing to another kind, not as something you do to others, driving them, jerking them around. It's for that reason nobody wants to dance with you." I could see in his eyes that he heard my words and understood in a new way what I was telling him.

I've worked with plenty of accounting firms over the years, all of them full of strong, gifted personalities who wouldn't have made it to the partner level if they weren't successful and good at what they do. Becoming a partner in a successful firm is a process that rewards such qualities. But in a difficult conversation, if you arrive showing off your strength and you push the conversation, you're likely to be unsuccessful. The stronger your personality, the more important it is that you learn to express yourself in a tentative manner so as to invite participation.

Of course, not everyone is overflowing with gifts of personal strength and charisma. The need for tentativeness may not be as strong for some, though anyone can get carried away in the heat of the moment during a crucial conversation and become passionately involved, perhaps emotionally out of proportion, and need to dial it down a bit. There are even times when a person's opinions or contributions to an important conversation may be undercut by tentativeness, particularly women who are too often talked down to, talked over, or discounted. In certain situations, some people may need to cast aside tentativeness and speak up forcefully for themselves. There are indeed times to exhibit confident strength, hiding any hint of a soft underbelly, in order to effectively compete in business or in life. In either case, tentativeness is an important and powerful tool that deserves thoughtful consideration.

Chapter 20

Dialogue and Discussion

When you speak of dialogue, most people think of characters talking in a movie or those sentences within quotation marks in a printed story. Actually, the word *dialogue* comes from the Greek word *dialogos*. *Logos* means "word" or "meaning," and *dia* means "through." In a sense, a dialogue is a flowing through of meaning. I like to take the translation a little further. In its most ancient meaning, *logos* meant "to gather together," suggesting an awareness of relationships. *Logos* might then be expressed as "relationship." I smile when I think of the way the book of John opens in the New Testament. "In the be- ginning was the Word." I now hear it as, "In the beginning was the Relationship."

Dialogue in a difficult conversation occurs when people think together in a relationship. Thinking together means you don't take your own position as final. You let go of certainty and consider possibility. Tentatively sharing in relationship with others, you discover puzzle pieces and possibilities that might not otherwise have been brought to light. The object of a dialogue is not to analyze or to express opinions or to win an argument. The proper goal is to suspend your point of view so you can listen to and consider other opinions. Your aim is to actively listen and tentatively share, and out of this healthy process, truth emerges unannounced, not because you have chosen it.

Conversations are sometimes like tennis matches, each side hitting their solid ideas and well defended positions back and forth. Such conversations can be called discussions. It may be heated or civil, but the core of discussion is debate. One synonym for discussion is argument. Discussion has the same root as the word "percussion" and "concussion," a root that connotes striking, shaking and hitting. A discussion is a banging of ideas. Always start a difficult conversation with dialogue and get agreement from all involved before moving to discussion. If one party thinks he's in a dialogue and the other is banging away as if in a discussion, one of them is probably going to get hurt, if not both. You don't have to challenge every thought. Make sure from a process standpoint that you collect puzzle pieces first. After the puzzle pieces, converse and discuss what is agreed upon as well as what isn't. You're going to wrestle about some things, but you're going to be candid with one another while in discussion mode. All parties in a difficult conversation must be on the same page and at the same stage from dialogue through discussion.

In the healthy process of difficult conversation, you create an environment in which you can collect puzzle pieces. You want to explore thoughts and feelings. You want to understand what the other party is saying. You actively listen and tentatively share what you're thinking. That's dialogue. As you collect puzzle pieces, at some point you're going to have to switch gears and move from dialogue to discussion, where you'll wrestle and debate with the other party. *You think that is the point? I think this is the point.* Of course, you'll want to wrestle graciously. How you say something is just as important as what you say. A healthy process is more important than any given topic under discussion.

Because you can't control how effectively others listen, you need to do your best to control how effectively you send your message. The very same words: *I can't wait to get to work*, will have a different implication depending on your tone of voice, in other words, your attitude—excited, bored, sarcastic, angry. The very meaning of the words you use can be shifted by your emotional tone. Something as simple as the word "really" can have a different meaning depending on your tone—sarcastic disbelief or delighted surprise. Imagine someone tells you he won the lottery. The way you say the word "really" will influence how he interprets your feelings about it—and maybe whether or not he shares his winnings with you.

Tone & Inflection

Meaning can also be affected by inflection, the way your voice rises and falls. It's something you probably don't think about when speaking, but inflection can be just as important as the words you choose when expressing what you want to say. Often, it changes the main idea of what you're saying. Beyond the exact meaning of the words you use, inflection indicates how you feel about what you're saying. "How did you DO that?" means something different than, "How did YOU do that?"

I didn't tell him you were stupid. (Somebody else did.)

I didn't tell him you were stupid. (It didn't happen.)

I didn't tell him you were stupid. (But I was thinking it.)

I didn't tell him you were stupid. (I told someone else.)

I didn't tell him you were stupid. (I was talking about someone else.)

I didn't tell him you were stupid. (I didn't say it in the past tense, because you're still stupid.)

I didn't tell him you were stupid. (I told him something else about you.)

The meaning of your words can change depending on which words you emphasize as you speak. Your meaning may also change based on your emotional tone. The misuse of tone and inflection can explain why sometimes people don't seem to understand you even when you use the right words and grammar. Be careful to manage your tone and inflection so you don't come across unintentionally hostile or all stirred up, which may hinder the other party's ability to hear your message. Managing tone and inflection can be an important tool for being more effective in difficult conversations. As you listen, reflect the tone you hear back at the other party. *You seem to be really upset about this.* Offer the other party the opportunity to realize and clarify. *No, I'm not upset. I'm just trying to bring emphasis.* Be candid but also gracious. Remember, you're trying to strengthen a relationship, not destroy it. The relationship is the heart of what's at stake. It can change your work environment, the success of your business or your marriage. If you want to strengthen a relationship through a difficult conversation, create an environment for healthy dialogue and discussion, and learn to manage your tone and inflection.

Chapter 21

Trust and Candor

Trust is an important relationship investment that can pay big dividends. In a business context, trust doesn't have to refer to an intimate way of relating. It's mostly about creating and inhabiting an environment where everyone feels safe to express their thoughts. As a professional, you aren't trying to make best friends with your colleagues, but you do want to create enough trust to effectively partner with them in a shared business model. Establishing trust with one helps engender trust with many.

Stephen R. Covey's book *The Speed of Trust* offers the powerful insight that trust can be developed and it can be eroded. Some people believe it's static—it's either there or it isn't, as though trust comes with an on-off switch. That's a faulty view. Trust is built up over time, and it's destroyed over time. In my consulting practice, I've witnessed too many situations in which a relationship has been strained to the point of breaking, and it negatively affects an entire business, and by the time I'm called in, the situation is thought to be hopeless. Trust has been destroyed and the situation is irreversible. But I know that trust is always destroyed in a particular manner for some specific reason. I know from experience that wounds can be salved and relationships salvaged. It doesn't happen all at once, but trust can be recreated as surely as it can be destroyed. It's always worth the effort of trying to restore trust, because not trusting people brings even greater risk than trusting them.

One of the ways trust can be built up is through effective listening, the ability and willingness to make room for others' thoughts and feelings. It's a powerful way of making a deposit into a relationship. Also, when you make a commitment, it's important to follow through on it. If you make a promise and fail to keep it, you undermine trust. Listen to yourself as well as others. Be faithful and keep your promises. Be genuine and share your thoughts in a gracious way. Don't be two-faced or false.

Trust can also be built through collaboration, which is another way to strengthen relationships. It requires a willingness to work with others, not through or around them. Of course, it's a lot harder than it sounds. Effective communication requires clear expectations. What you say and what another party thinks you said may not be the same thing. If you're thinking that you agreed to this while they're thinking you agreed to that, then your relationship is in danger. Invest the necessary time to clarify expectations.

An important aspect of trust is loyalty, not just the face-to-face kind, but even when the other party is not in the room. Be careful about duplicity. Own it when you screw up, and don't be afraid to apologize. In any relationship, trust can be destroyed when one side fails. Sometimes trust is ruined simply because one side refuses to acknowledge a mistake or won't apologize over an otherwise minor infraction. Apologies are important, as is extending forgiveness. I'm sometimes hired to deal with business relationships that have become frayed, endangering a company's business model. Often, I'm able to precipitate dramatic breakthroughs, and those frayed relationships end up stronger than ever. Clients have told me they look back on those moments when they were able to say, "I'm sorry" or "I forgive you," and they feel as if they'd somehow reinvented themselves, because the recreation of an important relationship helped them and their entire business to move forward.

You can overdraw a relational account by breaking trust—by not listening or by breaking promises, manipulating, being duplicitous, being harsh or abrupt, or by taking a win-lose approach. Such tactics are always at someone else's expense. When you violate expectations, when you're disloyal or full of pride and arrogance or hold grudges, trust deteriorates and relationships are frayed if not destroyed. Businesses fail for far less. Fortunately, trust can be developed and strengthened. It can be effectively taught and learned. I often teach clients the ways in which broken trust can be restored. Balance can be achieved through relational deposits of active listening, kept promises, honesty, kindness, courtesy, collaboration, clarified expectations, loyalty, apologies and forgiveness.

Candor is another important way to make a high-risk, high reward investment in a relationship. There are benefits to displaying candor. Defined as the state or quality of being frank, open, and sincere in speech and expression, candor speeds up communication and brings energy to a difficult conversation. It takes courage, but it's worth the risk. People tend to get more actively involved as space is made for candor. Some may think it best to avoid candor because it makes them uncomfortable or they are socialized against it, but the lack of candor can weaken a relationship or a business.

In my career as a management consultant, I've noticed one of the most overlooked business strategies is the use of feedback. It's often neglected, even though it can dramatically affect a company's performance. In a high performance business environment, core differentiators—those that set a business apart from others in the same market—can easily be eroded when feedback within an organization is stunted or done improperly. Poor feedback leads to the breakdown of process, a lack of efficiency, less communication, and underperformance. Effective feedback, on the other hand, always improves performance. It's important to capture feedback in an ongoing way, and candor should be used appropriately. Often, the open sharing of ideas is shut down when managers or leaders rely on blunt tactics that discourage open processing. Candor requires diligence, but speed and effectiveness increase when candor is present in a personal or work environment. A lack of candor can cause you to go around the same mountain over and over again. You become lost and blind to the clear warning signs that might otherwise direct you if you were open to them.

Many times, I've asked my clients, "Has the organization you run or work for ever told you candidly how they saw you, what you're good at, what you're not good at, where you are, or where you're headed within the organization? When was the last time you received an honest, straight between the eyes feedback session or company evaluation that gave you understanding about where you stood in the organization and what you needed to improve?" When I ask those questions, too often the answers are no and never. Businesses and organizations wrestle with providing such evaluations because it's hard to be frank. It's hard to speak the downside, though that's an important part of any difficult conversation. There's a cost to candor. It can be uncomfortable, but when others see you're willing to be vulnerable and candid, even though it might not feel good, it empowers them to be the same. I'm not saying be harsh. I'm talking about proactively saying what you're really thinking. You can do that graciously and at the same time not back away from the truth. Candor increases the speed with which one reaches the core of a problem. The conversation will be no less difficult, but it will be time-savingly direct.

Graciousness and candor are not opposites.

Years ago, I worked with an accounting firm that hired me to facilitate a strategic planning session. They were wrestling with questions of future growth and where they were headed as a firm. Did they want to struggle through the pains of change or just keep doing what they were doing? I'd done interviews with each of the partners and knew they were successful as a team. Individually, they each had a stable and comfortable life. For that reason, some of the partners liked things just the way they were. They were all from the South and benefited from a gracious culture and upbringing, typically genteel Southerners, which is to say not prone to public candor. They didn't always share out loud what they were truly thinking, not wanting to be too critical or unkind, as that was considered ungracious.

I did some training with them that spotlighted how important it was to get their real thoughts on the table. I started a conversation and facilitated a group discussion regarding whether or not the firm should reach to grow or hold fast to the level they'd already achieved.

Eventually, a couple of the partners broke through the barriers of gentility and began sharing what they were really thinking. They hesitantly revealed how frustrated they were. They spoke in a gracious way but were quite pointed in their observations and opinions. The firm's business model relied on attracting new talent, and they were concerned that some in the firm were too comfortable, laying back and not engaged in actively growing the business, which would ultimately undermine long-term prospects for the firm. Without naming names or casting accusations, they called out those who they felt were coasting, using words that were guarded and nonspecific. They used phrases like, *too many of us*, or, *some around here*. A couple more partners contributed input, and that seemed to empower the others to share. It became a courteous but vigorous discussion. There was more intensity and speed to the conversation, people ready and wanting to speak because candor had become part of the process. Once they began being candid with each other, I no longer had to draw them out. It was as though a door had opened and energy filled the room, inviting greater participation. It was powerful, and ultimately, they all got on the same page because they were able to hear and understand one another. They became even more pointed in their observations as they politely collected everybody's thoughts then debated various points of view and opinions. They decided as a firm that growth was a priority. In the best interests of the firm and for its long-term success, they agreed to change certain behaviors and individually take ownership for the company as a whole. Instead of coasting or resting on laurels, they decided they would each invest more time and energy by sharing their knowledge and experience with new hires. Together they instigated a plan to set the firm up for the future.

Common sense says you can't solve a puzzle if you don't have all the pieces. Without candor, things can remain hidden and you end up hopelessly trying to solve a problem without all the pieces of the puzzle. It's important to create an environment where all parties can be candid with one another, making puzzle pieces more readily available. Reality will settle into the conversation in a much more direct and intense way. That's powerful for personal relationships and for business organizations.

Candor can make people feel awkward, even dangerously uncomfortable. Sometimes you have to defend your perspective in a difficult conversation, yet you don't want to hurt the other party, and if you're blatantly candid, you might do just that. A part of you is afraid to be candid because of the effect it might have on someone else. But you have to get those puzzle pieces on the table or you won't be able to fully address the issue and solve the problem. Self-interest and risk of failure can make a person unwilling to fully engage, so it's important to create and sustain an environment where it's safe to be candidly honest, so puzzle pieces can be collected, with the problematic strains in a relationship uncovered and used to effect change and healing. That may sound warm and fuzzy, but it's also good business.

Before an organization can develop a culture of candor, it must examine the cultural rules that currently govern it. Cultural rules can run deep, and they typically resist change. An example of this can be found at NASA. The cultural ground rules that contributed to the *Challenger* explosion sixteen years earlier were still operating in 2003, leading to the *Columbia* shuttle disaster. The panel that investigated the causes of the *Columbia* tragedy went beyond the technical cause— a chunk of flyaway foam that damaged a wing—to blame an organizational culture where engineers were afraid to raise safe- ty concerns with managers who were more worried about meeting flight schedules than about risks. The head of NASA at the time, Sean O'Keefe, said in the aftermath of the Columbia tragedy that no employee who spoke up about safety concerns, even to outsiders, would be reprimanded in any way, but since 2003, NASA may have become even less transparent as a result of pressure put on political appointees to the agency in order to keep employees, including a NASA scientist concerned about global warming, from publicly expressing views not in keeping with current administration policies.

Relationships have to be grounded in reality. Healthy, productive communication requires you to be open to what others are thinking and feeling. You have to be willing to make room for others' thoughts even if you don't like or agree with them, and you have to be committed to saying what you're really thinking and feeling. It requires energy and strength to be candid, and it's necessary to do so in gracious ways. When grace and candor come together, it can be powerful. In difficult conversations, for strengthening relationships or team building, trust and candor are crucial tools.

Chapter 22

Forgiveness

Forgiveness can be defined as a conscious, deliberate decision to release feelings of resentment toward a person or group who has harmed you, regardless of whether they actually deserve your forgiveness. Forgiveness can be challenging, especially when the offending party offers either an insincere apology or nothing at all. However, it's often the healthiest path forward. Forgiveness allows you to acknowledge a wound, understand the other party's point of view, and process emotions in an unhurtful way. Forgiveness brings the forgiver peace of mind and frees him or her from corrosive anger. Although there is some debate whether true forgiveness requires positive feelings toward the offender, experts agree that it at least involves letting go of deeply held negative feelings. In that way, it empowers you to recognize the pain you suffered without letting that pain define you, enabling you to heal and move on with your life. There is extensive research tying physical health to the ability to let go of bad experiences, including what others have done to you. How many times have you needed to ask forgiveness? If you need it, so might others. Forgiveness is an important and necessary tool if you intend to successfully navigate intense, difficult conversations.

As a consultant, I've uncovered deeply strained relationships in which something happened long ago that was never talked about, never debriefed. I've discovered buried resentments ravaging the workplace environment, ruining effective communication, and stifling teamwork, all because of one party's inability to relate to another who has wronged him. Part of my job is to get to the heart of such problems. Through interviews, coached activities, and difficult conversation, the original offense is often revealed. Sometimes the offender will then say something like, *oh, well, I didn't mean that.* Or else, *I'm sorry you feel that way.* Neither is an apology that recognizes and accepts responsibility. *I'm sorry what I did had such an impact on you* is a better response.

There is an important difference between intent and impact. Say you reach for the peas and accidentally knock a glass of milk into someone's lap, and he looks at you and says, *why did you do that?* And you respond, *hey, it was an accident. I didn't mean it.* Okay, it's good that you didn't mean it, but your actions have resulted in a mess in the other person's lap. You should say you're sorry for what you did, whether you intended it or not. Accident or not, it's your doing and you need to own it. You need to make a true apology and accept responsibility for whatever you did or whatever part you played that had a negative effect on someone else.

Words are powerful. You'll never be able to partner or effectively work with others if you don't learn to incorporate the language of forgiveness. When someone shares with you that what you did had a negative effect, take the time to say, *wait. Let's pause right there. I want to apologize. That wasn't my intention.* Or if it was your intention, you might say, *you know what? I didn't mean what I did to have that effect. I handled that wrong. I apologize.* Apologies are powerful, and they are necessary if you wish to get to a healthy place in a difficult conversation.

> *Forgiveness does not change the past, but it does enlarge the future.*   —Paul Boese

True forgiveness doesn't require anyone to deserve it. Forgiveness is extended because the offended party needs to let go of corrosive resentment or ill feelings that hold him back. Some of the most important moments for apologies and forgiveness are when someone says something they wish they could take back. You may have said something in the heat of the moment that you wish you hadn't, or something you know you shouldn't have. The opportunity to apologize is important. The words, "I'm sorry" are healing and powerful for all concerned. Of course, it's also important and necessary, especially when someone apologizes, that forgiveness is extended. Choose to forgive so as not to let you heart get bitter. Let go, so you can continue to work productively together. Saying, *I forgive you* is different than I *trust you*. Trust is earned and built over time. You can choose to let go and forgive, knowing there may still be work to do in your relationship. It doesn't mean everything's fixed, but forgiveness is an important step nonetheless. Your ability to move on and grow is hindered if you hold on to unforgiveness. Learning to let go of past offenses is important to the future of any relationship.

Chapter 23

Unmet Expectations

A major underlying reason for conflict with others is unmet expectations. I can't overstate this. Most difficult conversations are about unmet expectations. What I've often found is one party had a sense about what was going to happen, and because it didn't, that party became upset. The other party's expectation was completely different, and because the parties never clarified their expectations, they wound up having to work their way through a difficult conversation. When each party in a difficult conversation identifies what their expectations are and in what ways they are being unmet, it can frame a healthy environment for collecting puzzle pieces.

I worked with a family business, a beverage distribution outfit that was transitioning within the family to a third generation. Most family businesses don't make it from a first generation to the next, and an even greater percentage fumble the handoff from the second generation to a third. Families that have been in business—or businesses that have been in the family—for a generation or longer often seek assistance in effectively passing the torch. I was brought in to help the beverage distribution outfit set up the incoming generation for success and to strengthen the communication between generations. The patriarch asked me to help him evaluate his children's readiness and ability to take over the business. He'd inherited the business from his father, who he felt had treated him poorly by making him work long hours with low pay, but he'd managed to dramatically grow the business and now he was expecting the same of his children. His main concern was his oldest son. He and his son weren't working well together, so I was brought in to facilitate the difficult conversations that were necessary. Family dynamics can make such conversations even more difficult. The oldest son expected the transition to be a cakewalk, a done deal. His taking over was a no-brainer and would be no problem. He felt he could do the job in his sleep. He didn't see the need to work the floor or work his way up some silly ladder of seniority. He was insulted by the idea of long hours with little pay and didn't expect to waste his time struggling into a position of authority. The father however expected his son to work and suffer in the same way he had for his father before him. He worried his son didn't have the ability or work ethic to grow the business the same way he had when he'd taken over. They each had different perspectives about the business and completely different expectations regarding what it would take to manage it.

I saw immediately that both sides needed to share their perspectives and voice their expectations, so I facilitated a series of conversations and I prepared an environment in which they could say things to each other that had not been said before. Emotions were frayed, as was the relationship between them, but I was able to referee and coach them in the art of difficult conversation. It was painful for both parties, and sometimes I had to call a timeout because of tears and recriminations. The son felt his father didn't trust him and so didn't love him. The father felt his son was shirking responsibility and therefore endangering the family legacy. At times, each found it hard to continue. That's when a third-party facilitator comes in handy. It took months of difficult conversations, but I got them to a place where they were able to hear each other and bridge the gap between their different perspectives. Once expectations were clarified, I initiated a personal development plan for the son, which included some challenging tasks that tested his leadership abilities. The son discovered he wasn't as ready as he'd thought, and his respect for his father's accomplishments increased. Their conversations weren't only about transitioning the business. They wrestled with the dynamics of father/son relationships and parenting techniques, and most of all, expectations.

Puzzle piece collecting will bring unmet expectations into the open as one side or the other realizes they are playing from a different playbook. Puzzle piece collecting will do that. Understand how often unmet expectations drive the strain in a relationship. That insight can help you spot trouble before it rears its head.

Chapter 24

Pressing Through Difficulty

Difficult conversations are, by definition, difficult. The necessity to press through that difficulty is paramount. The hope that healthy process will guide you to the other side is equally important. When a conversation feels most difficult, most uncomfortable, chances are you're at the brink of breakthrough. In those moments, it's crucial to lean in and press through. Maybe what's being shared is painful. Maybe there are negative emotions roiling inside you, but if you don't stay with it, you'll never gain the result you are hoping for. The ability to press through discomfort is a vital skill. Maintaining faith that healthy process will get you there is also crucial and will feed your ability to press on. When things are most intense, that's usually a sign that you're at a critical point. It is necessary to push through and out the other side of difficulty. Give up too soon, and it's all for nothing.

I was once hired by a large accounting firm with eighteen partners, one a particularly high performing individual who came across as dismissive, difficult to work with, full of himself, as though he thought he walked on water. He was completely oblivious to the effect he was having on the staff and other partners, but he was so high performing, his numbers so fantastic, that no one wanted to confront him. I was brought in to help the firm's performance, not to specifically address the problems caused by this particular partner, but I quickly discovered that the relationship between him and the others was broken, and it was negatively impacting the firm's performance. I interviewed all partners and staffers, and each revealed that this guy was a problem, though none wanted to go on the record about it because he was something of a golden god. He was so powerful due to his high performance that if he decided to turn on someone, that person would be toast. Everyone was afraid of him. When I interviewed him, it was clear he was so out of touch with himself and others that he had no idea anyone had a problem with him.

I decided to bring all the partners together, and I introduced an exercise that I wanted them all to participate in. It was an exercise I'd learned from *The Five Dysfunctions of a Team* by Patrick Lencioni. It worked like this. One person sat in a chair in the middle of the room while the others took turns sharing something about that per- son that really helped the group, as well as something that person did that worked at cross-purposes to the group. Whoever was in the chair was not allowed to respond, only listen. Afterwards I debriefed each person and helped them to process whatever was shared. I'd spent some time setting ground rules and framing the activity in a way that created a safe environment, so when it was the high performing partner's turn in the chair, the others were comfortable enough to be direct about the way he came across to them. The criticisms were accompanied with compliments, but the criticisms were pointed and sharp and unavoidably true.

At the end of the exercise, after the others were released, I spent some quality time with the high performing partner. He was devastated by what had been shared. He was trying to process the idea that his business partners didn't like him. He realized that meant the same was probably true of everyone else at the firm, maybe others in his life as well. He was overwhelmed to hear that he was a jerk, and everyone knew it but him. He was a high performing partner, late in his career, yet no one had ever been so directly critical of him, because they were afraid of him. It was a painful moment for him, and powerful. He could have argued, denied, or simply fled from the awful truth. Instead, he looked inside himself and pressed beyond the awfulness and admitted he didn't want to be that person, that jerk. He asked me to help him change, and I provided him with tools to strengthen his self-awareness. I offered him insight into how to be sensitive to the ways in which he affected others and to proactively ask whenever he wasn't sure. Difficult conversation brought him to a place of painful truth. He was overwhelmed at first, but we did a lot of talking over a lengthy period of time. He made a commitment to change, and he truly did. His partners and colleagues noticed and appreciated his efforts, and it positively impacted the performance of the entire firm.

Breakthrough comes from pressing through.

I can't tell you how many times I've felt I wasn't getting any- where in a particular situation, one in which I'd been called in as a consultant. I'd hit an impasse. It just wasn't working. It was awkward, uncomfortable, and there seemed no way forward. If I'd stopped and given up working through those difficult moments because they were painful, or I just couldn't see the light at the end of the tunnel because I didn't yet have all the puzzle pieces, then I wouldn't have so many testimonies of success. It's powerful what can happen with the right process and tools, but understand, you will come to a place in a difficult conversation that you will want to run from or fight against. You may feel like ripping the face off the person across from you, or you might want to flee the room, but you have to press into the difficulty, stick with healthy process and trust it. In the moment, it won't feel good. You'll want to stop, but don't. Lean in. Press on. Success and health are on the other side. Learn to press through those painful points and see them for what they truly are—stepping stones that can take you where you need to go.

Give serious thought to the use of a third-party facilitator to help you press forward and through. You might wonder whether two people having a difficult conversation really need a referee, but it's something to consider if at all possible. Like a marriage counselor, a third party holds all sides accountable and helps focus a difficult conversation, keeping everyone on track when one party gets emotional or the other starts to run off on a tangent. A third party in a difficult conversation can focus on process so the other parties can fully participate.

A facilitator can also objectively spot key points that need to be addressed more deeply.

The important duties of a third-party facilitator include observation, feedback, and directed questions that can focus the conversation and keep the process on track. A third party can help engender a safe environment for collecting puzzle pieces. Keep in mind, the facilitator should be someone both parties have confidence in. If one of the parties believes the facilitator is going to take sides, turning the conversation into two on one, that will ruin any chance of success. The facilitator has to be someone both parties agree upon, not someone who tries to help one side win. An effective facilitator is someone dedicated to protecting all parties and keeping the process on track while honoring the relationship above all else, someone who gives feedback and forces reflective listening into a difficult conversation without driving the conversation. A good facilitator focuses on process, making sure all parties follow the six-step model. A facilitator might steer a difficult conversation by saying things like:

Do me a favor and restate what you just said with less antagonism or in a more gracious way.

Let's not avoid what we have to talk about, but let's use caution and slow the conversation down.

Paraphrase what you just heard the other party say.

You're trying to fix the problem, but it's a little early for that. We're still collecting puzzle pieces.

Where does that thought come from? Can you share an experience to support those feelings?

Let's spend a little more time digging deeper on that topic.

Let's use candor, but make sure we stay gracious.

Chapter 25

Addressing Underlying Trauma

Most of us have experienced moments of profound emotional pain in our lives, traumatic experiences that can influence our developing worldview. Our worldview might be inaccurate or unhelpful, and when we find ourselves again in a similar circumstance to that which caused our original pain, we may have a hard time managing our re- actions. For some people, a harsh father or a domineering mother— common dysfunctional family dynamics—can set a tone that makes it difficult to relate well to strong personalities. Uncomfortable feelings from a painful experience, either physical or emotional, may be re- awakened during a difficult conversation.

Over the years, I've been hired countless times to help a struggling business with personnel issues. At some point, more times than you'd believe, I'll instigate a difficult conversation between feuding parties and quickly discover an unusual level of pain in the conversation, often because the issue at hand isn't the true issue needing to be addressed. There is something simmering beneath the topic on the table. One of the parties seems traumatized, not from the recent event we're trying to process, but from something painful in the past. There's obviously more to the issue, something more that needs to be addressed. In such a situation, I'll stop the conversation and call a timeout to go one-on-one with the wounded party. I'll encourage that person to take some time to examine his or her feelings and mine down to process the pain. I'll suggest he or she find someone to talk it through with, and then we can pick up the conversation later, be- cause without the true issue being identified, a difficult conversation is merely impossible. We'll never be able to break through or reach closure.

Not long ago, I consulted for a large accounting firm with ten partners. They were in the process of identifying emerging leaders and choosing which ones to promote. There was disagreement about some of the candidates. People were sharing their different thought processes and having a reasonable discussion until one young man's name was brought up. The conversation quickly got heated. There were strong opinions all around, but one of the female partners had a strongly negative response, which caused others to push back at her— *It's an easy choice. The named gentleman deserves it. Why all the fuss?* The discussion became antagonistic, so I called for a timeout. I found a private space to sit one-on-one with the woman partner who was objecting so strongly. I asked her to help me better understand her thoughts about the promotion process and the candidate under discus- sion. The intensity with which she was communicating made me think something more was going on. The woman and I already had a good relationship. I'd worked with her before and there was history between us, so I was able to gently prod her into opening up. Seemingly out of nowhere, she revealed that she'd suffered a traumatic experience as a young woman. She'd been abused by a man whose personality was similar to that of the candidate up for promotion. He reminded her in subtle ways of her abuser. As her tears flowed, it became apparent that the issue for her was not the issue under discussion by her partners. For her, it was tied to a previous event she'd never shared with anyone. Our private conversation opened old wounds, but it also paved the way for future healing. I advised her to seek counseling and talk out her experiences with a trained specialist. It was freeing for her to see that her objections about the candidate up for promotion had little to do with him, who he was or what he had done or not done.

In difficult conversations, especially when there is a great deal of intensity, the issue at hand often isn't the true issue. Something else may be going on and you have to dig it out and deal with it in order to breakthrough and get to the other side. Most lives have brokenness and trauma in them. Some people have pain that's never been dealt with or properly processed, and a difficult conversation can make it feel as though someone is pressing directly on a pressure point, reawakening the pain. In the course of collecting puzzle pieces, hidden traumas are sometimes uncovered. It's often necessary to address underlying issues, traumatic events that may be weighing heavy on someone's heart, before a difficult conversation can continue or come to closure.

Undoing Catalytic Events

I've often had to force clients to deal with things that happened long ago, events or interactions that impacted an important relationship but were never processed. One party may have walked away from the pain or confusion and just written the other party off. Often neither party remembers exactly what happened, so I push them to dig deeper and look for puzzle pieces. When did the relationship fall apart? What contributed? What do you remember about the time of year when it all broke down? What did you feel and experience? What were the key takeaways for you from that incident?

It is difficult to go back to a place of pain or confusion, especially if you believe nothing good can come from a revisit, but if a relationship is frozen and not functioning, it's necessary to find the initial sticking point in order to unlock it. Many times, the catalytic event happened weeks or months or even years earlier, but it was painful and continues to negatively impact the relationship. Because the two parties never processed it, they are now having a hard time working together. Their relationship has been strained for so long, both parties feel it's always been so. As I facilitate a difficult conversation between them, a specific event or interaction is brought up, and it becomes apparent that it was the catalyst for everything that has gone wrong between them. Something in the past has had a profound effect on one or both parties, but at the time, they ignored it, thinking they'd just get over it. Both parties may even think they have gotten over it, but deep resentments remain that make it difficult for them to interact anymore. There are some pain points that, if you don't truly get past them, they can ruin a relationship. They need to be talked about so they can be processed, so healing can take place. When that happens, relationships can be strengthened and even restored.

In my experience, it's rarely the case that someone wakes up in the morning thinking about how to ruin somebody else's life, but the truth is, it's not uncommon for a person to do something that inadvertently messes with a colleague's career. They never talk about it together, never process it, and years later, it has become an infected wound that has completely destroyed their relationship. They can't be in the same room together. It's affecting their ability to do business, and now the powers that be have to consider letting one of them go, even though they're both good workers with great skills. This is where a third party can come in handy, someone to lead them effectively through a difficult conversation, uncover dormant puzzle pieces, and help them process and heal. And here is where forgiveness may be- come an important factor. One party reveals, *hey, when you did that, it really hurt me*, and the other party owns it by saying, *I had no idea what I did had such an effect on you. I'm sorry.* And when *I forgive you* arrives, you find yourself consoling a couple of wet eyed executives with quivering lips. Of course, just because somebody says, *I'm sorry*, and somebody else says, *I forgive you*, that doesn't mean everything is hunky-dory, but it's amazing how much it can clear the air and prep an environment that can heal and strengthen a relation- ship, even get an organization or business back on a productive track. Difficult conversations can uncover puzzle pieces that reveal catalytic events that need to be processed. Handled appropriately, damage can be undone.

Learning to Be Okay

When things around you are strained and others are losing their heads, and maybe blaming it on you, it's necessary not to panic. Just because a situation seems out of control doesn't mean you have to be. Learning to be okay is an essential, though difficult, skill to develop. I believe an important aspect of managing your heart comes down to that very thing, learning to be okay. It's important to be good at difficult conversations, but it's essential in life to learn to be okay even when things around you are not. There will always come troubling times, things you can't control or didn't expect. For some, the tendency is to strike back at whatever is provoking or threatening. For others, the tendency is to bolt, to get out of there. In business, as in life, it's important to manage what's going on inside you so you can keep processing and relating to what's happening around you, even though it doesn't feel okay, because it's not okay. But you *are* okay and things *will be* okay if you can lean into the difficulty, come up with a game plan, and effectively deal with it. Running from trouble will only exhaust you and get you nowhere.

Life throws curveballs and challenges, no less in difficult conversations. All too quickly, things may get intense. It can involve discomfort. It can involve risk. Concurrent with pressing into difficulty, it's important to learn how to be okay when difficulties come your way, because they will. Learn to manage your thoughts and feelings. Learn to be okay, even though it doesn't feel that way. Being an effective leader, an effective manager, an effective relationship builder requires you to process and not run away when difficulties arise. Consider the motivating words of Rudyard Kipling in his inspirational poem, reminding us of what it is to truly be a man.

If *by Rudyard Kipling*

If you can keep your head when all about you
Are losing theirs and blaming it on you;
If you can trust yourself when all men doubt you,
But make allowance for their doubting too;
If you can wait and not be tired by waiting,
Or being lied about, don't deal in lies,
Or being hated, don't give way to hating,
And yet don't look too good, nor talk too wise:

If you can dream, and not make dreams your master;
If you can think, and not make thoughts your aim;

If you can meet with Triumph and Disaster
And treat those two imposters just the same;
If you can bear to hear the truth you've spoken
Twisted by knaves to make a trap for fools,
Or watch the things you gave your life to, broken,
And stoop and build 'em up with worn-out tools;

If you can make one heap of all your winnings
And risk it on one turn of pitch-and-toss,
And lose, and start again at your beginnings
And never breathe a word about your loss;
If you can force your heart and nerve and sinew
To serve your turn long after they are gone,
And so hold on when there is nothing in you
Except the Will which says to them: "Hold on!"

If you can talk with crowds and keep your virtue,
Or walk with kings, nor lose the common touch,
If neither foes nor loving friends can hurt you,
If all men count with you, but none too much;
If you can fill the unforgiving minute
With sixty seconds' worth of distance run,
Yours is the Earth and everything that's in it,
And, which is more, you'll be a Man, my son!

PART THREE

Maintaining Healthy Relationships

Chapter 26

Heart Posture

You may have heard Barbara Streisand sing *People who need people are the luckiest people in the world*. Her voice is certainly beautiful, but the first time I heard that song, I immediately questioned its sentiment. Needing people isn't something that makes me feel lucky. It makes me feel vulnerable, which can be quite uncomfortable. What really makes me feel lucky, blessed even, is a sense of connection.

Life is about relationships—with others, with ourselves, and with the world at large. An effective way to heal, strengthen, and maintain those relationships is through the process of difficult conversation. The most efficient way to manage such conversation is by utilizing emotional intelligence. Look at it the other way around. By strengthening your emotional intelligence, you become more efficient and effective at difficult conversations, which are a crucial means of strengthening and maintaining relationships, which are essential for business and for life. That's it in a nutshell, the thesis of this book. It could probably be reduced to a few commonsense commandments: Know yourself (the only way to truly relate to others) and maintain balance between your inner needs and your outer goals. Don't be a rude jerk. Show respect for yourself and others. That may sound simple but it's not. Transforming yourself from who you are into who you should be, who you want to be, is no easy feat. You have to dig deep.

Say you have an apple tree in your yard, but the apples it bears are bitter. What do you do? You might decide to pick the bad apples and get rid of them, do away with the problem, but next season, the same bitter apples come back, because you haven't fundamentally changed anything. So, maybe you decide to prune the tree, cut off whole limbs until you've completely rid the tree of its ability to bear bad apples. If you have any experience with fruit trees, you know that pruning doesn't ultimately result in less apples. It eventually brings more fruit, and next season, you're not only going to get bad apples, you're going to have a whole lot more of them. You're wasting time and energy because you're attacking the problem at the fruit level, when the true problem is in the root system. If you want to rid yourself of bitter fruit, you have to get to the root of the problem.

Managing your heart, as well as your ability to lean into difficult conversations even when it doesn't feel good, means you have to dig all the way to the root of your belief system. Real change doesn't happen at an external level. Because relationships are at the heart of every-thing, let's review some of the aspects of emotional intelligence that allow you to get to the root of problems that keep you from healthy, fruitful relationships in your business and in your life.

Too often, we plug ourselves into a business model, or perhaps we find a comfortable place within a family or some other personal relationship, and that role becomes our focus. Yet we've already es-tablished that people are more important than any business model or assigned role, so our goal should be to relate well to others by placing them ahead of our personal or professional agendas. The irony is that personal and professional agendas are more efficiently achieved by placing others first. That's the nature of healthy relationships. They thrive when they flow from a proper posture. I don't mean the set of your shoulders or the tilt of your chin, but rather, your inner attitude, the alignment between your heart and your mind. When your heart is aligned and open, you're able to make room in the middle of your life, in the center of your heart, for others. It can make you feel vulnerable and uncomfortable, and obviously you need to maintain balance while putting others first, but you have to be willing to share space in your life. Individuals quickly pick up on those who are in it for themselves.

It turns people off and shuts down connections, making genuine relationships more difficult. Making room for others shows you value them. You have to be willing to move from a self-centered position. Step outside your worldview and allow others to occupy, even momentarily, the center of your attention.

I won't lie. It's not easy. In fact, the stronger your personality, the more successful and confident you are, the more difficult it can be, but if you want to succeed at relationships, then you need to be good at connecting with others. Being other centered facilitates healthy connections and productive relationships.

> *No one cares how much you know, until they know how much you care.* —*Theodore Roosevelt*

The quickest way to connect with people is to do something nice for them. Look for opportunities to serve others. Service leadership is a powerful way to accomplish strong personal connections. Think about it. When someone comes to you needing or demanding something from you, it's instinctive to be defensive. *What do you want and why?* But when someone approaches with a heart posture that says *What do you need and how can I help?* it bridges distances and lowers walls so connections can happen. Servant leadership is more than just kind actions. It's a heart posture and a powerful tool for building and maintaining relationships.

At the same time, it's important to cultivate a teachable attitude, one that says, *there's much I don't know but nothing I can't learn.* Being teachable means having the ability to learn new things and the willingness to admit there are things you still need to learn. Never arrive with a know-it-all attitude. That allows no room for others, and so, no room for a relationship. Posture yourself as someone willing to learn, not just for the sake of posturing, but because it's true. Be genuine. One of the joys of being in relationships is learning about other people. There's much to glean from life and from others. Be open to that and remember there is a difference between knowing and agreeing. You want to learn so you can understand, even if you don't agree. Create an environment with room for others' thoughts and feelings and perspectives, so you can collect puzzle pieces and move deeper into difficult conversations. Take a teachable posture and you'll receive more helpful feedback, which allows you to strengthen your relationships so you can be more effective in your life and career.

Chapter 27

Building Empathy

Perhaps the most effective EQ component for purposes of difficult conversations and relationship maintenance is empathy—the ability to understand the emotional feelings of another. I've mentioned the importance of self-awareness—working to understand ourselves, our belief systems, and what makes us tick—but just as important is the need to be other centered, which means working to understand others. There are three basic types empathy. *Cognitive empathy* is understanding someone's thoughts and feelings in a rational rather than emotional sense. *Emotional empathy* is relating to someone else's feelings so strongly that you literally feel them too. *Compassionate empathy* is understanding someone's feelings and taking appropriate action to help.

People too often use the words *empathy* and *sympathy* interchangeably, though they don't mean the same thing. Sympathy is mostly about observation and an acceptance of what someone else is going through. It can amount to feeling sorry for someone, which is an acknowledgment of a situation. It doesn't require you to experience the emotion that the other person is going through or even fully understand it. Sympathy is a valuable trait, but it doesn't always lead to substantial action. Instead of a sympathetic statement like, *that must be frustrating*, an empathetic reply can resonate more with a customer, colleague, or employee. *I understand how you're feeling,* means you're experiencing a fraction of the other person's emotions or feelings because you see things from their perspective.

Daniel Goleman, author of *Emotional Intelligence*, describes empathy as the ability to understand others' emotions. He also says, at a deeper level, it's about defining, understanding, and reacting to the concerns and needs that underlie others' emotional responses. This makes empathy a key component of emotional intelligence and an important aspect of difficult conversation. It's how we understand what others are experiencing. Empathy goes beyond sympathy, beyond feeling *for* someone. Empathy is feeling *with* someone through the use of understanding and imagination. It's a connection, a link between self and others, in other words, an important part of healthy relationships. Empathy involves a shared perspective, not necessarily that you care, just understand. To share in someone else's perspective, you have to put yourself into his position, imagine yourself as him in a particular situation. You can't empathize with an abstract or detached feeling. You need to have some knowledge of who a person is and what he is doing or trying to do. As John Steinbeck wrote, "It means very little to know that a million Chinese are starving unless you know one Chinese who is starving." Empathy is about acknowledging your biases and stepping imaginatively into someone else's shoes. This can be difficult, but it gives a unique perspective that can lead to positive action taking. Feeling empathy comes more naturally to some, but mostly, it's a choice. You can choose to view things from other perspectives and try to see things with others' eyes. True empathy gives you a chance to experience real growth by allowing you to feel different emotions and take on new and unique viewpoints. It provides an opportunity to experience and understand different cultures and ways of life. Empathy prepares you to deal with cross-cultural differences by broadening your perspective and deepening your sense of connectedness.

People often refer to the Golden Rule—Treat others as you would like to be treated yourself. It's a good rule and worth remembering, but sometimes differences in world views and general assumptions about life can dramatically impact the way we treat others. I never intended to dishonor or offend my dinner hosts in Japan, but differing perceptions and understanding about the use of chopsticks—what each of us viewed as norms—left a chasm between us that caused offense. Perhaps we need another rule: Treat others the way they like to be treated, which means investing time to better understand the needs and expectations of others.

Sometimes the way we perceive the world is influenced by our cognitive biases. For example, we may attribute other people's failures to their internal characteristics, while blaming our own shortcomings on external factors. Such bias makes it difficult to recognize all the factors that contribute to a situation and make it less likely that we'll be able to see the situation from the perspective of another. It's not always easy or even possible to empathize with others, but through people skills and imagination, you can work towards more empathetic feelings. Research suggests individuals who empathize enjoy better relationships and a greater sense of well-being.

It's worth repeating—empathy involves understanding others, not just feeling what they feel. You can empathize and still disagree with what's being said. It's difficult to empathize when you disagree, but it's a necessary skill in order to be effective at relationships. One of the best ways to grow in empathy is to be an effective listener. Empathic listening is a major component of healthy relationships. It's takes a deliberate heart posture to strive to understand why others think as they do, what they're feeling, where they're coming from, and why they act as they do. If you can learn to live outside your own head and embrace other perspectives, your thoughts and ideas will become even more vibrant, diverse, and, ultimately, strengthened. So, listen actively, ask questions, and be curious.

Reserve Judgment

And while you're keeping an open mind, remember to keep an open heart as well. Resist making critical judgments prematurely. Even in my sixties, I recognize sensitive areas in my life that still surprise and confuse me. If I'm not an expert on what's going on inside myself, how can I presume to be an authority on others? My point is, resist

making judgments about why or what someone else is doing. It's okay
to have thoughts about others' motivation, but don't jump to conclusions. Too often we make unfounded assumptions, deciding another
person's motivation prematurely. This can damage a relationship and
prevent healthy dialogue. In a difficult conversation or a strained relationship, if you say, *I know what your problem is. You're selfish,* then
you've declared a final conclusion that can stifle further communication and even destroy a relationship. Resist judging the motivations
of others. It's okay to have thoughts and opinions, and maybe your
opinions are even accurate, but don't close your mind or your heart.
Don't rush to judgment until you've talked it over with the other party.

We rarely know the full extent of what others are going through,
so we need to be careful not to arrive at an overly quick verdict regarding anyone else's behavior and not ascribe motive to that behavior
without first conferring with that other person. When we come to a
place of judgment, our hearts tend to harden. That hardness can get in
the way of effective listening and puzzle piece gathering. Sitting in
judgment is no way to move forward. Be open to the fact that you may
not have the right idea or proper perspective regarding what motivated someone else or why events happened the way they did. Don't
jump to conclusions about others before you've conversed with them
and listened to their perspectives, their motivations, and explanations
about what's going on inside them. You're not even an authority on
everything going on inside your own self. You're learning things all
the time, or should be, about yourself, about ulterior motivations and
the exact way you're wired. It's a lifelong process. If you're not done
working on yourself, what could ever make you an authority on what's
happening in someone else's life or heart?

Reserving judgment doesn't mean you can't talk or share or bring
your concerns about what someone else has done into the conversation. Expressing disapproval is one way to collect puzzle pieces. But
express yourself graciously and tentatively, because you want to invite
participation and because you're still open to learning, not closed off
or sitting in judgment.

I previously mentioned catalytic events. Imagine a colleague does
something that profoundly and negatively impacts you, and you

believe he did it on purpose. In fact, you know he did it on purpose and you decide he's a jerk, so you go out of your way to avoid him. It's two years later, and you still have no desire to be in the same room with the idiot, but perhaps intervention, either as divine intercession or as an order from a supervisor, forces you into an uncomfortable conversation with the fool. And you realize you never really talked about it with him, so you call him out for being such a jerk, and he says, *jeez, I didn't mean it that way. That's not what I meant to happen. I'm sorry I did that.* And suddenly, a relationship that hasn't been a relationship for two years is now something different, something new and pregnant with possibility. My point is, for the same reason it's necessary to be tentative and gracious with your feedback, it's important to be cautious with your judgments.

Look for Opportunities

Your investment in a relationship requires you to deposit into it and allows you to make a withdrawal from it. The way you respect, the way you treat, the way you relate to others can be either a deposit or a withdrawal. Sometimes you need to express that others are important even when you don't need something from them. An important part of any relationship, business or personal, is the opportunity to smile, to say hello, to affirm and respect others. Every interaction counts, and people can tell when you're faking it. In a work environment or a family dynamic or just among friends, be careful not to get lost in your own world and miss the opportunity to connect with others, even when you're not asking anything from them. The more aware you are of others and of yourself, the better you'll be at relationships.

When I was in high school, my older brother was away at college, and he'd periodically call home to ask my parents for help covering tuition or the cost of books. I remember sitting at the dinner table when my brother's latest call came in. Everything was fine, and my dad promised to send a check in the morning, but when he hung up, my dad shared an amused eye roll with my mom and said, "Typical. He only calls when he needs money." I remember thinking then that when I went off to college, I'd be sure to call home sometimes for no reason, just to check in and say hello. I didn't like the idea of my parents rolling their eyes whenever I phoned home.

Too often, we only think of investing in others when we need something. We go out of our way to be nice to someone if there's personal gain or a favor we need. We don't always consider how an everyday interaction can affect the condition of an overall relationship. We make relational withdrawals all the time. It's important to make routine deposits as well, to go out of our way to connect, smile, and be kind to those we interact with. Otherwise, the strain of withdrawals can damage a relationship. People want to, and should, feel important in a relationship. How you interact with them determines that.

Chapter 28

Commitments and Confidences

Whenever you do interact and connect, be careful about the commitments you make. Don't say yes to someone, even if you feel obligated in the moment, if you don't have the intention or capacity to follow through. When you say yes or no, mean it. While making decisions, think about how it will affect your relationships. Sometimes, saying yes is more difficult. Other times, saying no is more important. Some find it easy to say yes but hard to follow through. Some are quick to say no. Either way, consider your commitments and follow through. Others will be counting on you. Drop the ball, and it will impact your relationships. In fact, it can even destroy them. In relationships, you may have to step outside yourself and commit to things that are uncomfortable. It may take a bit of life stretching. Make room for that but think it through. Make meaningful choices. Consider what's best for a relationship before you commit, then be sure to follow through once you do. Let your *yes* be yes, and your *no* be no.

Along with your commitments, honor confidences. Breaking a confidence has the potential to ruin a relationship, and the way you handle information shared from a place of intimacy is important to more than the immediate relationship. Other people are watching the way you honor and respect shared information. If people don't trust you, they won't share with you. You'll end up on the outside, disconnected. If you break a confidence with a party over there, it's going to dramatically affect your relationships over here, because people are going to be skittish about what they share with you.

Respect Boundaries

It's important to respect boundaries as well. For that, you need to apply wisdom. A helpful way to clarify personal and professional boundaries is by understanding what you are responsible for and what you are not responsible for. Often, boundaries are crossed when someone feels obligated, personally or by others, to own something that isn't theirs to own. It's unwise to accept every perspective or opinion from others as truth, just as it's foolish to expect others to accept the same from you. Respect where people are coming from, be open to different perspectives or ideas, but don't try to take ownership of everything that passes your way. You'll burn out or lose yourself in the process. If you don't own what you need to own, and if you don't allow others to own what they need to own, you're going to fail at relationships. Know the boundaries of what's yours and respect the boundaries that others perceive. Don't take ownership of things that others are responsible for, and don't shirk responsibility for things that are truly yours.

Remember science class in high school, permeable cell membranes? Permeable describes the way things pass in and out of a cell. But if everything slips in, the cell will die, and if everything slides out, the cell will also die. Same for relationships, particularly with regard to difficult conversations. You need to exercise wisdom regarding what to let in and what to let go of. You have to recognize and respect boundaries. Don't take in everything as truth, and don't repeat or pass along everything that is shared. Choose the right environments and the right people. Accept information, words and feelings, but receive it all with the proverbial grain of salt. Don't indiscriminately down- load or upload everything that's offered.

Manage Time

Your most valuable commodity is time. Invest it wisely. Keep it in mind as you work through your busy schedule. Be willing to invest your time in the relationships that are most important. The more difficult a relationship, the more time it takes to reinforce or mend it. Yet, when things are strained, the tendency is to pull away, to withhold time and energy. Every relationship, easy or hard, requires some investment of time. Use some of your precious time to evaluate your relationships, whether with a challenging teammate in a business context or with a needy teen in a family context. Make an inventory of the minutes and hours you spend with those you love. Does the time you're investing reflect your value system? If not, adjust your schedule.

Practice Self-Control

How are you at managing your emotions, your time, and your tongue? You'll never be able to manage others if you can't manage your own heart. The better you become at managing yourself, the better you'll be at influencing others. I've already mentioned the problem of managing emotions and how challenging they can be to control in a difficult conversation. In a relationship, it's crucial that you manage what's happening inside of you. If you want to thrive in relationships, and trust me, you do, then you need to manage yourself. Don't just blurt your thoughts or feelings. Control your mind and heart, your tongue and your actions. Be careful what you share and how you share it. It's not a single, onetime lesson. It takes a lifelong commitment. If it were easy, we'd all be a lot better at it.

Be Self-Aware

Self-control requires self-awareness, which has been deemed the highest correlating attribute to effective leadership. Self-awareness is an important component of EQ and the life's blood of successful relationships, and it's good for business because leadership is about influence. If you're out of touch with the effect you have on others, you won't be able to control or manage it or them. Self-awareness is being in touch with that effect. It's being in touch with what you do well, what you don't do well, how you come across to others, and how you impact them.

The key to developing self-awareness is to ask questions. Ask your friends, your colleagues and coworkers, your family and friends what they think of your performance as a businessman, as a team leader, as a sibling or a spouse or a parent. Accept and learn from their feedback. You might not always agree, nor should you, but their perspectives will provide great data points for growth. The more open you are to input, the more self-awareness you'll gain, which fosters stronger relationships and more opportunities for leadership, resulting in greater success in business and in life.

Chapter 29

A Family Is a Team That Requires Leadership

Succeeding in business can make life less stressful at home. The reverse can be true too. A rich personal life can help focus and strengthen your efforts at work, but you shouldn't have to sacrifice one for the other. Everything is connected. The components of emotional intelligence can impact both your personal and professional relationships, and it's necessary to seek balance.

I married at a young age. I was twenty-two, my wife, twenty-one. Starting out, our marriage was predictably wonderful, founded on great friendship and deep trust. We were committed to one another and things seemed to flow smoothly and easily. Six or seven years into the marriage, something shifted. Nothing drastic, but our relationship, which used to come so naturally, began to require effort. We had to work harder at it. That was when I began to understand the impact my emotional intelligence, *or lack thereof*, was having on our connection. I didn't have the framework or the vocabulary to describe emotional intelligence back then, but now I'd say that my social skills and empathy were high. My self-regulation and self-awareness, however, were disastrously low. It was mostly my lack of awareness that caused discord. What I thought was smooth sailing led to pent-up frustration for my wife.

I now know the greatest challenge to a marriage is not one's spouse. It's the weight of one's own perspective. We enter into a marriage-type relationship carrying a mental model of what it will be, what it should be. Consciously or subconsciously, we base our roles, our way of relating to one another, even our value systems on what was modeled in the parental relationships we observed growing up. Trying to blend two separate perspectives makes for a precarious dynamic. Our mental model may be profoundly different than that of our significant other. It can take a lot of work to create a new, shared model, but without self-awareness, it's even more challenging. I based my expectations of my wife's role in our relationship on the behaviors I observed in my mother, and I subconsciously modeled my behaviors on my father. Consequently, I considered it perfectly normal and completely acceptable for her to take care of all household responsibilities while I found self-indulgent ways to unwind on the weekend—sports, reading the newspaper, hanging out with friends, things I felt entitled to do after a hard week. The whole time, my wife was thinking, *when is it my turn to kick back?* Fortunately, when the tension between us grew great, we were wise enough to seek help. Through a third party, we were able to find ways to identify and talk about our unmet expectations and how disappointment was affecting our partnership. I still remember my shame when it was pointed out how clueless I was. It was painful, but powerful. Not only did that process help develop my self-awareness and overall emotional intelligence, it strengthened my marriage.

Marriage-type relationships require not just a commitment to learning each other's perspectives. They are about honoring one another through those differences. Key components of EQ include self-awareness and self-regulation, knowing and understanding what is going on emotionally inside and having the ability to regulate the responses and behavior pushed by that emotion. When my wife and I first clashed on perspectives and role definitions, I wasn't very good at regulating my reactions. Nothing tests one's ability to self-regulate like conflict, and as most partnered individuals know, conflict and the potential for offense are a daily part of life. Trying to find an agreed upon model for living together takes many difficult conversations.

How you regulate yourself in those conversations can have a lasting effect. Emotional outbursts can destroy a relationship over time. The greater your ability to delay self-gratification and put the needs of your significant other in front of yours, the stronger your relationship will be. Keep in mind, regulating your emotional responses is not the same thing as stuffing your emotions.

Part of self-regulating your emotions is learning to talk about your feelings in a healthy way. Being vulnerable with your partner about your emotional state is vital to a healthy relationship, but it's important to share feelings without letting emotions run the show. This is tied to the EQ component of empathy, one's ability to understand other perspectives. There is always some level of disparity between world-views in any relationship between two people. When two people enter into a deep relationship, the issue of empathy can be profound. The key to strengthening empathy in a partnership is through the effort of seeking to understand where your partner is coming from. Instead of waiting your turn to interject your view into a conversation, ask questions that will allow greater understanding of your partner's view.

Marriage, like business, like life, is about commitment. In order to meld separate worldviews and thrive in relationships, all parties have to be committed to shared, long-term goals. Developing the EQ component of self-motivation is key to pressing through the difficult conversations that inevitably come. In the short term, conflict doesn't feel good. No one enjoys being told they are wrong or that their way is not in fact the only alternative to the highway. Being motivated to work through differences, for the larger goal of a strong and healthy relationship, is key. In the thick of a conflict, your motivation is not going to come from your spouse or partner. You'll have to find that motivation within yourself and rally around a larger goal. If you are committed to a relationship, EQ skills are not only important but imperative. If all you want is to coast through any commitment as long as it's enjoyable, well, this isn't the book for you. If you lack empathy, self-regulation, motivation, or self-awareness, it isn't too late to develop those traits.

Developing emotional intelligence is a great way to strengthen relationships, and marriage is a perfect proving ground for developing

EQ. Today, the concept of the nuclear family has shifted. Many children live in blended or adoptive families, many with one parent or in a generationally extended family. The very idea of family is expanding, and with it, the aftermath of unhelpful stereotypes. It's hard to miss the effects of patriarchal clichés, young men given the impression, or sometimes blatantly told, that they have to be always strong, that emotions are a sign of weakness, that money defines them, that women are things they're entitled to. Such false ideas too often obscure the truth—that happiness isn't tied to how many people you can control or how many Benjamins you have in your bank account. Happiness is tied to one's ability to build strong, healthy relationships. It's tied to the strength of family bonds and the friendships in your life. Happiness is critically linked to the way you relate to others and the impact you have in the world. In other words, happiness is directly related to emotional intelligence.

I'm a parent. It's the greatest blessing of my life and the greatest responsibility. I have six children, and no, it's not a competition, but as a parent I want to see my children safe, happy, and successful. If you're a parent, I'm sure you do too. In order to get them to that place, we have to work against stereotypes that we ourselves may have been influenced by. Women are most often viewed as nurturers, so men can sometimes feel awkward talking to their children about emotional and social processes. I know. I'm a dad. We have to push past that. Our children are watching us. They're watching their moms too, of course, and as parents we're each equipped to speak about our own experience. Our children are watching the way we navigate relation- ships, the way we prioritize career and family, and the way we chase our goals. I encourage you to be confident in the way you support and strengthen your children's emotional intelligence. Start by making sure you understand it yourself. And realize, your children are paying more attention to your behavior than to your words. Strengthen your own EQ, and model it. Here are four foundational truths that I've found helpful for modeling and raising emotionally intelligent children.

Encouragement Should Be Partnered with Challenge

Challenging your children can sometimes seem at odds with your efforts to encourage them. It's important to find the right balance between affirming and correcting. If you only spend time affirming and never correcting, your children won't learn to handle the reality of the world. At the opposite end of the spectrum, if you only challenge and never affirm, you will most certainly fray if not break the parent-child bond. How do you strike the right balance? Constantly look for opportunities to make investments in your children. Praise them for the things they do well but be careful to affirm them for who they are as well as what they do. Then, when the time comes to correct or challenge them, don't be shy. When your kids feel safe and secure in their relationship with you, they won't be crushed when you challenge them. When you affirm or discipline your kids, make sure you do it in a healthy way, so they truly receive it. Every child is different. Keep in mind that what is meaningful to you may not be meaningful to them. Learn how your children are wired and meet them where they're at.

Self-Awareness Is Key to Success

Once again, self-awareness—understanding who you are, what you do well and what you don't, understanding how you impact others and working to manage that impact—is an important life skill to develop in your children. To help your children grow in awareness, they need feedback. Help them realize that other people have perspectives and thoughts that can be helpful, perspectives they should actively seek out. Talk to them about the value of listening to what their peers, teachers, coaches, and others have to say about them. Emphasize that at times, feedback can be taken with a grain of salt, but it should always be considered and weighed before throwing it out altogether. It takes maturity to be open to feedback, and it can take a while to get there. Learning to value feedback is a process that requires guidance along the way. Help your children to develop an appreciation for feedback, and model that appreciation in your own professional and personal relationships.

Processing Failure Helps to Problem Solve Challenges

Life is not always fair and certainly not always easy. Help your children by teaching them to lean into and process challenges. As a parent, you want to protect your kids from problems, and although it's understandable, protecting your kids from every little thing doesn't help them in the long run. You don't want a challenge to overwhelm them or induce fear and anxiety, but you do want to provide them with the opportunity to see a problem through to the end, so help them process their emotions and failures, help them to get to the root of the problem and talk it out. Often, kids see failure as a fatal thing. We know it isn't. Failure is an opportunity to learn from mistakes and rise above circumstances to greater success. If you do not take the time to dialogue about these things with your kids, they may give up too early and never build the perseverance they need to be successful in future challenges.

Listening Fosters Empathy

You want your kids to understand that people have different perspectives, different beliefs, and different histories. Listening to other perspectives helps your kids to strengthen their empathy. It's important that they relate well to others—when it's easy and when it's not. To emphasize the importance of listening, you need go no further than your own mirror. Two ears, one mouth. Public schools train the mouth and the mind more than they train the ears. You can model empathy to your kids by listening to your loved ones at home. Show your kids active listening by asking reflective questions and making room for the answers you hear. Let your highest achievement be the platform your children stand on. You may not feel confident at first. If you weren't taught emotional intelligence as a child, don't panic. It's never too late to learn and grow your own EQ. Don't get stuck in the past. Read books, seek counsel, get coaching, and pursue growth in emotional intelligence.

It should be obvious that your efforts to relate to your family at home are much the same as what is required in your relationships with your colleagues and with the teams you lead at work. Learn from past failures and move forward. Make a commitment to your kids, your coworkers, your teammates or your employees. Show up and lead by example.

Chapter 30

A Final Note of Encouragement

Life is a journey of self-discovery. As we learn about the world and the way it works, we learn also about ourselves. We learn of our needs and desires and the reasons for them. From our reactions to the world we gain insight into our own capacity for hope and love, for fear and shame. We learn who we are, maybe even who we might be- come, from the people and events that inspire us, as well as those that threaten to harden our hearts. It's no little miracle that our self-under- standing grows exponentially as we come to understand and empathize with others. Which is the key to building and sustaining healthy relationships.

One more time, say it with me. Relationships are everything.

How you relate to others, and how they relate to you, lays the groundwork for success in all areas of business and life. Developing and strengthening the components of your EQ will feed your rela- tionships, and in turn your relationships will help grow your EQ. Difficult conversations, necessary and inevitable, are an important part of establishing and maintaining healthy relationships, and they are managed more efficiently through the use of EQ. In turn, your EQ will be strengthened by the process of difficult conversation. Healthy relationships, emotional intelligence, and difficult conversations, they

feed and are fed by each other, so don't wait to be proficient at one before beginning work on the next. Open yourself up to the fundamental
nature and truest purpose of life. Healthy relationships are strengthened through the process of difficult conversation, which support and
are supported by the components of emotional intelligence, which in
turn help to establish and strengthen healthy relationships.

I encourage you to build and strengthen the relationships in your
life. Work to repair those that are strained. Use and develop your
emotional intelligence. Engage in difficult conversations. Lean in. Be
deliberate and courageous. Be open to feedback and learn from
experience. Practice and grow stronger, and don't give up. Healthy
relationships are the goal. Emotional intelligence and difficult conversations will help get you there. Keep in mind the essential rules: Don't
be a rude fool. Show respect for yourself and for others. Apologize
when necessary and choose your battles. Don't assume the problem is
other people. It might very well be you. Don't turn every little thing
into an argument but have the courage for difficult conversation when
necessary. Continually work on your communication and social skills.
Know yourself and maintain balance.

You can do it. Start now. Whatever tools you don't have, you can
develop. You are your own first and best resource. Get to work and
keep at it. I wish you good luck and every success.

PART FOUR

Appendix: Checklists & Worksheets

NINE REASONS DIFFICULT CONVERSATIONS ARE SO DIFFICULT

1) Difficult conversations put us at risk.

People are hardwired to have a negative emotional response to risk. Flight or withdrawal is a common reaction, which is why most people choose to remove themselves from dangerous or risky circumstances. Of course, this is not helpful in difficult conversations.

Certain personalities love risk. Some adrenaline junkies will jump into risky situations without caution or wisdom, which can work against effectiveness just as much as withdrawing. Learning to manage your risk response is critical to effectiveness in challenging conversations.

Ask yourself, *what is the risk I am feeling? Where is it coming from?* Strategize ways to manage that risk. Do this in preparation of a difficult conversation. Most off-the-cuff responses are not helpful or effective.

If you find yourself suddenly thrown into a difficult conversation that involves risk, you may need to call a time-out and reschedule the conversation in order to prepare more effectively.

2) Difficult conversations involve a level of uncertainty.

Life is full of uncertainty; and we must learn to embrace it. We don't know where a difficult conversation will end up, but even if the conversation does not go well, there is still a lot that can be learned from it.

Difficult conversations are full of uncertainty. They are also full of insights and paths to places we have never been before. Commit to leaning into that truth and embrace life as an adventure.

3) In difficult conversations, the issue under discussion is rarely the issue at the heart of the matter.

Conversations can get complicated in a hurry. Often, we think we know where a conversation is headed, but difficult conversations rarely go as planned. Be ready for that. It's important to maintain a heart posture that allows you to follow where a conversation leads, which is only possible through the power of listening. Explore what every participant is thinking and feeling. Collect puzzle pieces and navigate accordingly.

4) Many of us have witnessed only faulty models of argument and discussion.

Too few people have ever witnessed a healthy model or experienced a healthy process for difficult conversations. Most of us grew up in homes with faulty models for handling difficult conversations, either fight (loud arguing or disagreements aren't allowed, and violence may be part of the process) or flight (we don't talk about difficult things, don't have difficult conversations).

5) We may find it hard to get outside our own perspective or worldview.

All of us look at life through different lenses. We look through the lenses of our experience, upbringing, culture, and socioeconomic position.

People effective in relationships understand that their perspective is just that, a perspective. They are open to examining their own and looking at alternative perspectives. Leaders and managers must be able to look at and constantly evaluate their own perspectives. They also need to be willing to be part of conversations that challenge their paradigms. That approach is crucial to healthy process when conversations turn difficult. Accounting for other people's perspectives is an important part of difficult conversations.

6) We struggle to be candid and say what we really believe.

Candor is not the same as tactlessness. Learning to be gracious while being candid is very helpful to being effective in difficult conversations.

Candor, the open sharing of ideas, is crucial and involves courage, particularly if you grew up in a home where your voice was not nurtured. You may need to work to rise above that circumstance in order to grow in candor, which can help you grow your self-confidence.

7) We are poor listeners.

Many of us have been trained in how to communicate our ideas, but few of us have been trained in how to listen. Effective communication is not just telling but listening. It takes focus and energy to listen effectively.

The skill of listening is not difficult: the heart posture to use those skills is the difficult part.

Listening skills are the keys to collecting puzzle pieces. People often think that a difficult conversation is unsolvable. It may be unsolvable without all the puzzle pieces, but when all perspectives and issues are on the table, it is amazing how solvable a puzzle can be.

8) We do not handle our negative emotions very well.

Negative emotions derail effective conversations more than any other barrier.

Self-control is a difficult skill to develop. Managing emotions may be the most challenging part of any difficult conversation. It can be a complicated, risky, and painful endeavor.

Managing emotions doesn't mean stuffing them, nor does it mean vomiting them all over the conversation.

9) Our insecurities arise.

Everyone needs security and acceptance. We all want to be loved, accepted, and to feel worthy, but often in difficult conversations sensitivities related to identity come up. It's hard to manage our hearts when insecurities arise.

Strong personalities often have the hardest time facing their insecurities.

Difficult conversations are difficult by nature—but it's import- ant not to give up. If you seek the results of genuine breakthrough in difficult conversations—increased understanding, rapid productivity, stronger team unity—it is vital to address the roadblocks in your life that threaten your success.

MY SIX-STEP MODEL FOR DIFFICULT CONVERSATIONS

One: Recognize the Problem

Be proactive to understand when something is not right and needs to be talked about. Waiting for a problem to go away or until it blows up will not work.

Step Two: Choose Appropriately

Find the right time, the right place, and the right participants for any difficult conversation. Properly frame the conversation, and remember, it's the relationship that you are fighting for, not victory in the argument.

Step Three: Collect Puzzle Pieces

The problem isn't that there is no solution. The problem is not having all the puzzle pieces to solve it. Create a proper environment to collect puzzle pieces.

Step Four: Manage PIE (Perspective, Insecurities & Emotions)

Make room for others' perspectives. Manage your heart and remember that expressed emotions dissipate.

Step Five: Stay on Track

Manage process, not just content, and keep in mind that the issue under discussion may not be the true issue.

Step Six: Come to Closure with Consensus & Accountability

It's not enough just to be heard. There needs to be some mechanism for implementation and accountability. "I am sorry" and "I forgive you" are important words that may need to be spoken.

DIFFICULT CONVERSATION PREPARATION CHECKLIST

Name:_____

Relationship:_____

Area of Conflict: _____

_____

BEFORE THE CONVERSATION

Step One: Prepare

What are you feeling and thinking that makes you want to have a difficult conversation?

_____

_____

_____

What type of conflict is this?

A. Unmet Expectations. What expectations are you disappointed about?

B. Ongoing Relationship Strain. When did you first feel the strain? Why?

C. Recent Event (Acute). What is your perspective of the event?

_____

_____

_____

What story do you tell yourself about the other person that may hinder your ability to fully engage in healthy process? Write down your assumptions.

_____

_____

_____

Step Two: Pick the Best Time, Place, and Frame

When is the appropriate time to have the conversation? (Time of day, day of the week, etc.)

_____

_____

_____

Where is the appropriate place? (Look for neutral territory where everyone can feel safe.)

_____

_____

_____

Who else should be involved? Who might be a healthy third party (not taking sides)?

_____

_____

_____

What is the appropriate frame for the relationship and the conversation?

_____

_____

_____

What is the best way to start the conversation? (Plan out your first 1–2 sentences)

_____

_____

_____

What are words/phrases to avoid?

_____

_____

_____

DURING THE CONVERSATION

Step Three: Collect Puzzle Pieces

Build an environment that invites the other person's thoughts, perspectives, and even contrary ideas. Bring reflective listening into the conversation, even if the other party does not understand the power of listening.

Helpful comments for collecting puzzle pieces:

- You and I see this issue from different perspectives. I would like to better understand your perspective.

- What do you see as contributing issues/thoughts/perspectives to our conversation?

- Let me try and summarize what I have heard you say.

- What are the key points you hear me saying?

- Is there anything you are thinking that you are not saying?

What are some thoughts that you may have a hard time bringing to the table? List them below and make a commitment to share them while you also search out the other person's perspective.

_____

_____

_____

Step Four: Manage P.I.E.

Manage Perspective

Have you already diagnosed the problem and solution before the conversation has begun, or are you going into the conversation with an open mind, actively seeking other perspectives?

Examine Your Perspective: What are the holes in your viewpoint?

_____

_____

_____

What might be the other person's perspective? How might you see from their point of view?

_____

_____

_____

Manage Insecurities

Where do you feel most vulnerable in your life? How might this conversation touch those areas?

_____

_____

_____

Are there any broken places in your heart that are being stomped upon in this conversation? What other insecurities may arise in this conversation?

_____

_____

_____

Manage Emotions

What is making you feel (fill in the emotion) right now?

_____

_____

_____

Step Five: Keep on the Path

Questions to keep in mind in order to guide the conversation:

- What are you trying to accomplish?
- Is there a better way to do it?
- Do you feel like the conversation is on track?

Never attack or allow the other person to do so. Try to move forward together. Make room for emotions, but don't let them dominate.

What do I need to apologize for? What do I need to forgive?

_____

_____

_____

AFTER THE CONVERSATION // NEXT STEPS

Step Six: Plan Moving Forward

What do we agree on?

_____

_____

What do we disagree on?

_____

_____

What is the real problem?

_____

_____

What are the potential solutions?

_____

_____

Which solution is being proposed; accepted; and implemented?

_____

_____

WHO will do WHAT and by WHEN?

_____

_____

What will be different as we move forward?

_____

_____

_____

What communication, meetings, actions, items need to happen as a follow-up?

_____

_____

_____

How do we make sure there is accountability to what has been agreed upon?

_____

_____

_____

PRINCIPLES OF EFFECTIVE FEEDBACK

Giving Candid Input

You can't control how effectively others listen, but you do have control over how effectively you send your message.

When possible, prepare your message to assure good communication.

Be candid, direct, specific and honest

Use easy to understand language.

Do not allow emotions to control your communications.

Focus on the nonverbal messages being sent.

Be nonpunitive in your communication.

Be other centered.

Ask for feedback from the other side to assure understanding.

Receiving Input

Be open. Teachability is a sign of maturity

Listen to feedback without getting defensive. If you find yourself getting defensive, ask yourself, why?

Do not blindly accept feedback as the ultimate truth. Let it in and give yourself some time to think about it.

Paraphrase the feedback to be sure you really understand what the other person is saying.

Remember, all feedback is good, because it gives you valuable information about how others think and feel.

Feedback can lead to identifying areas of potential growth. If you receive it well, you will get more of it. We all need input, even when it doesn't feel good.

ABOUT THE AUTHOR

John Chisholm earned his degree in psychology from the University of Illinois, Champaign, in 1978. He has been married for 41 years and has six children and 12 grandchildren. For the past 24 years, John has been a successful business consultant, mostly for accounting firms and family-owned businesses.

ABOUT JC CONSULTING

Strategic Planning: John has facilitated over 250 strategic planning sessions with various sized businesses, using his special skills to design effective processes that engage participants to embrace challenging conversations during the development of strategic plans.

Conflict Resolution: When colleagues have a falling out, it negatively impacts a company's strategy and culture. If leaders grow to dislike or mistrust one another, it puts the entire company at risk. John's skills have proven effective at unlocking conflict, rebuilding trust, and reknitting broken relationships, resulting in transformed partnerships and increased productivity.

Succession Planning: John is experienced at using aspects of business strategy and conflict resolution to build strategic programs that deal with all of the complicated issues of succession in privately owned and family businesses.

Executive Coaching: John engages, challenges, and strengthens key leaders so they can better manage people, process, and performance. He primarily focuses on executives and emerging leaders as well as those in transition to higher levels of responsibility.

About Hiring John for Speaking Engagements

Public Speaking: John has a passion for sharing lessons learned from the profound journey he has been on for the past 30 years, including personal accounts and successful strategies for unlocking conflict and building healthy relationships. His stories of breakthrough while using the tools of emotional awareness and difficult conversations are encouraging to the human heart as well as practical for sharpening tools to build working relationships in all aspects of life.

John@johnchisholm.com